Donated by

ME
NA

McKINLEY ELVAS
NEIGHBORHOOD ALLIANCE
Serving all of East Sacramento

the Swell

dressed party

Other books by Cynthia Rowley and Ilene Rosenzweig:

Swell: A Girl's Guide to the Good Life

Home Swell Home: Designing Your Dream Pad

Swell Holiday

the Swell
dressed party

Cynthia Rowley and Ilene Rosenzweig

ATRIA BOOKS

New York London Toronto Sydney

ATRIA BOOKS

1230 Avenue of the Americas
New York, NY 10020

Photography by Lee Clower

Design by Chandler Tuttle

Illustration by Chico Hayasaki / CWC International, Inc. (http://www.cwc-i.com)

ISBN: 0-7434-4278-4

First Atria Books hardcover edition May 2005

10 9 8 7 6 5 4 3 2 1

ATRIA BOOKS is a trademark of Simon & Schuster, Inc.

For information regarding special discounts for bulk purchases,
please contact Simon & Schuster Special Sales at 1-800-456-6798
or business@simonandschuster.com

Manufactured in the United States of America

To Diego, a born Swell party boy.

Enormous thanks to the Swellest guys we know—
design genius Chandler Tuttle, sharpshooter Lee Clower,
as well as big daddies Rick, Bill and our agent David.

Contents

.the imperfect hostess

nobody does it better

Hostessing is a high-wire act, filled with thrills and spills. You're performing for a lot of people. Everyone's watching. The expectation is to do it flawlessly. But the secret is, no one really wants that. If an acrobat prances gaily along the wire, she'll get a round of soft applause. But for the big bravos, you need that . . . misstep that makes the audience gasp with anticipation to see how—and if—she'll recover her stride. Only then does the crowd offer their thunderous cheers and a standing O.

At least that's the rationalization of the Swell Hostess. Her party fantasy life is not filled with per-fec-tly seared filets of beef. The Imperfect Hostess reaches her entertaining heights with twin mottos: can-do and make do. On either end of her balance pole are the homemade cake and camouflaged take-

The party paradox at the heart of this book is that the Imperfect Hostess is not a renunciation of elegant entertaining but a return to it.

I

out, the fine china and a snip-and-rip tablecloth. She works fast and loose, mixes high and low, and doesn't worry about having the exact equipment. A wheelbarrow in the backyard makes for a great roving bar, champagne flutes excellent bud vases—and vice versa. She can deal with disaster—with her charm and wits. If the soufflé is teetering dangerously, she's got the Good Humor truck on speed dial—and can sweet-talk the driver into swinging by for an emergency dessert lift.

A party at its best is a place to be a little larger than life—funnier, prettier, bawdier—and the Swell hostess at her best sets the stage for her guests to try a few high-wire moves of their own.

The party paradox at the heart of this book is that the Imperfect Hostess is not a renunciation of elegant entertaining but a return to it. Other books show their model party planners mid-craft, rolling origami napkins, or in the garden plucking lemon verbena, but never at her own party shaking up fun. Yet a swell hostess is neither caterer nor kitchen drudge. Her quick fixes and fast solutions free her up for oft-overlooked more glamorous hostess duties—looking dishy, spending time with guests, running to the basement for the pogo stick. She's as crucial an element as the food and drink. So drop the denim work shirt and grab the tiara—even if it's for a barefoot BBQ in the backyard.

The Imperfect Hostess knows that the key to throwing parties with maximum style and minimum stress is having a focus. Not trying to be all things to all people. A Swell party is like a diamond, albeit in the rough. No two are exactly alike. The secret is making *one thing great.* A bartender flaming cocktails. The

swimming pool brimming with beach balls. Pickup lines being passed with the hors d'oeuvres. You looking like a billion greeting guests with a magnum of champagne in hand and a Polaroid camera around your neck.

The ticket to making a party colorful is not necessarily a big labor-intensive theme. 1001 Moroccan Nights! Just give 'em something to remember. And find inspiration in your limitations. It can just be that you don't have a dining room table in the new apartment yet, or that the backyard's a dump, or you have no time to cook. That's when you come up with the big ideas: cardboard boxes pushed together as a banquet table with tulips in the paint cans—the Not-Yet-Moved-In dinner party no one will forget.

The Swell definition of a party is *life elevated.* And it can happen at any time of night or day. The parties in this book go from a morning tag-sale brunch to a bachelorette blowout that could last till daybreak again. A Swell hostess is an equal opportunity partier, looking for ways to amp up the biggies— birthdays, showers—and celebrate small everyday occasions, too—a hangover brunch, adding a touch of swellegance to must-see TV night, or indulging an après-party impulse to invite everyone back to your place, even if it means claiming it was "the maid's day off."

For the big bravos, you need that…misstep that makes the audience gasp with anticipation to see how—and if—she'll recover her stride.

Whatever her shortcomings, The Imperfect Hostess shines at the party skills that matter most: loosening people up and drawing them out. To that end, she puts her energy and charm into sparking conversation and fanning flirtage, and she is not above whipping out enough games and activities for a five-year-old's birthday. Anything to make the bad times good and the good times unforget-table. A party at its best is a place to be a little larger than life—funnier, pret-tier, bawdier—and the Swell hostess at her best sets the stage for her guests to try a few high-wire moves of their own.

Now which way's the bar? This drink's getting warm.

1

early birding

breakfasts, brunches, morning-afters

type-ADD brunch

Ahhh, brunch—the ultimate Sunday luxury. Q-time to spend decompressing with friends, chitchatting gaily over flutes of mimosas, waiting lazily for the eggs Benedict to materialize. Who can sit still that long? Some of us can never really relax into a Bloody Mary stupor without a welling dread of the day slipping away—there are places to go, newspapers to read, cartoons to watch. The Swell remedy for the ADD hostess is to marry brunch with a morning activity you'd want to do anyway. Just because it's a party doesn't mean you can't accomplish something!

9

Tasty Tag Sale

Get rid of your old junk and hang out with friends while waiting for customers, some of whom might even be cute and single or have kids the same age as yours. Besides, why not make some dough instead of just eating it?

Invite

This is one party where you can't have too many guests. We evited friends to set up a "boutique" and sell their own stuff—or just browse and breakfast. Then we put our energy into making new friends by posting notices on trees and electrical poles advertising our tag sale and muffin tasting.

Simply offering food and drink elevates the tag sale to party status.

Setup

To make your event more guest-friendly than the typical junkyard sale, organize the merch into boutiques spread out over the whole yard so there are different places to browse and hang out. Best to get a head start the night before, since the hitch to this party is that it starts *early*. The hard-core tag-salers will be at your door ready to inspect your wares at the crack of dawn.

We created a "living room" from the bookshelves, reading chair, lamps and games for sale. Sales tables covered with cloths or bedding gave the yard a more soignée vibe, and helped sell the sheets faster. We dragged the stereo-for-sale to the stoop and cranked tunes. Cynthia figured out a way to display all the clothes and shoes in our fashion boutique without a rack of any kind just using a single oak tree: sweaters on hangers on the boughs, shoes around the roots, bags and hats thumbtacked into the bark and a full-length mirror leaned against the trunk. This was one occasion when Ilene's bad habit of wearing clothes with the price tag hanging off the back came in handy.

Sips and Nibbles

Simply offering food and drink elevates the tag sale to party status. Even the most minimal refreshments awe strangers and friends with your gracious hostessing and genius marketing strategy.

Lemonade Squeeze: Cynthia figured out a way to move a difficult item: single, unmatched glasses. We loaded a table with everything from a lone Austrian crystal flute to a Snoopy tumbler, and a sign: FREE LEMONADE! (GLASSES $1) Ilene made pitchers accessorized with strawberry or basil for added value.

Jammin' Muffins: It seemed tacky, even for a Swell girl with her mind on her money, to resell donuts and croissants from Sam's Club, though the margins were good and it did cross our minds. So for eats we went with a breakfast bake sale theme, a table of semi-homemade muffins and breads. We loaded up on those five-for-a-dollar mixes and, to make the corn muffins less dry, turned them into Jelly Muffins by filling the muffin tins halfway with mix, then adding a dollop of preserves before pouring in the rest of the batter. The other treat was Yard Sale Banana Bread, an old family recipe from Ilene's health-food childhood baked in two super long (18-inch) bread pans that, when laid end to end, were as long as a—yardstick. For good measure, we laid a yardstick beside the bread for customers, or guests, to help themselves: a dollar an inch.

Action

We could have made more money. But the sale took on gale force by eight in the morning. And we were still wandering around in a need-coffee coma, half dressed, our "boutiques" bare, no food out, and so much for our plan to put cute price stickers on the items with little product details. "Prada pumps ($3), excellent for chasing buses in Milan."

So we improvised what to charge on the spot and learned we had some very different retail strategies. Cynthia followed a fire-sale plan of unloading everything with prices that were, like New York retailer Crazy Eddie used to say, *"in-sane."* Ilene had a reverse-snobbery philosophy that people want to spend

more so they think they're getting better value. Cynthia proudly showed up with $30 saying she'd sold ten rugs. Ilene raised her eyebrows; she'd been selling them for $10 each. As one might suspect from Cynthia's years of experience, our fashion boutique rocked ($1 a pair of shoes if Cynthia was selling them; $5 if Ilene was tending shop).

The tag-sale brunch paid off. We made new friends—a TV producer who said he was interested in doing a Swell party show, and an arty dude who was just the part-time contractor we were looking for. Admittedly, we were too crazed to spend much time with pals who stopped by. But Ilene did make enough money to buy pool patio furniture with the proceeds, so next summer we can invite everyone to come and just hang out, maybe have brunch or something.

More Busy Brunches

Misery Loves Company—The Hangover Brunch

When everyone's had too much fun the night before, rather than endure morning-after misery in solitude, keep the party going. The Hangover Brunch is an ideal plan when you know a big night is in store and there'll be cause for recuperation and partiquing. There's no cure for "the mean reds," as Holly Golightly called the ailment, but you can find solace in the quiet company of fellow sufferers.

Recovery Room: The morning after a bender, set the room up in soft comfort. Put out slippers, soft throws, lots of pillows from the bedroom for crashing in the living room. On the coffee table set out a tray of Tylenol packets, bottles of Vitamin Water and iced eye packs. Lower the blinds.

Breakfast Pizza: Perfect hangover food, easy to serve, fun to eat and a more civilized version of the cold pizza you used to eat the day after a blowout back in college. You can buy the ready-made crust at the supermarket, top it with scrambled eggs, sprinkled cheese, and all the other omelet fixings for toppings. Crumble bacon on top and bake at 375° until the pie looks pretty, the cheese melt-y and the crust golden. An excellent dish for customizing, breakfast pizza can be half mushroom, half spinach, and people take the slice they prefer. You don't end up making seventeen omelets for eight cranky friends. You need that like another hole in your head.

Bloody Marys: A Swell hostess must know how to mix up a pitcher of the classic hair-of-the-dog drink. Originally invented at Harry's New York Bar in Paris as a "restorative" cocktail, it was named after Mary Pickford, the silent film star who, despite her nickname, "America's Sweetheart," must have really known how to tie one on. There are a million variations: more lemon, less pepper, hold the horse-radish—you have to make one to your taste. The one that suits ours is half V8 and half tomato juice with celery salt on the rim.

Animated Brunch—Saturday Morning Cartoons

Remember how much fun it was to wake up and watch cartoons all morning? Yeah, last weekend was pret-ty good! Why not invite a few friends to join in your regressive sloth? They can wear feetie pajamas, fuzzy slippers and sit as close to the TV as they like.

Shake Up the Sugar Shack: This party starts at the supermarket, indulging that childhood fantasy of loading the cart up with every cereal you've ever wanted: Cocoa Puffs and Cap'n Crunch, Frankenberry, Lucky Charms and all those promotional ones—The Hulk, Scooby-Doo!—your parents never allowed. Throw in some Grape-Nuts for any weirdos who might straggle in. Line up all the colorful boxes on the dining table or buffet. Put prizes inside, grown-up ones: lipstick, a Virgin Records or manicure gift certificate, costume jewelry. Serve mini milk cartons chilling in a big bowl of ice. And OJ in kid-size juice glasses. Cut up fruit toppings: bananas, berries, peaches, raisins—to meet FDA requirements. The hostess wears Mickey Mouse ears and has *total* clicker control, though you might consider DVDs of older cartoons if you don't want to get stuck watching Teletubbies.

This party starts at the supermarket, indulging that childhood fantasy of loading the cart up with every cereal you've ever wanted.

Media Bistro

Just spent Saturday night gabbing yourself hoarse, do you really feel like more small talk on Sunday morning? Brunch can be just having friends over to do what you really want to do: sip coffee and read the papers. A time to recharge the mental and conversational batteries.

Paper Chase: Get all the papers—from the Times to the Star to the Herald Tribune—fodder for celeb gossip, fashion criticism and political crossfire. Xerox *The New York Times Magazine* crossword puzzle so everyone can have a copy. Put out a mug of sharpened pencils. The brainiac who finishes first wins a subscription to the *Weekly World News*.

What a Spread: A good old Sunday morning bagel buffet, classic as the Gray Lady. Give the spread a homemade feel by whipping up your own cream cheeses: a salmon, a vegetable and a few unorthodox flavors they scorn in New York, like chocolate chip and cinnamon raisin. Do up a tray of NY deli garnishes: sliced cucumbers, tomatoes, bread-and-butter pickles—anything but onions.

Caffeinate: You can't compete with Starbucks, so don't try. Go pre-Starbucks with an urn of hot stuff alongside flavored whipped creams—Irish-coffee style. A small bottle of Baileys will sweetly heat up the cups and the political debate. Have a pitcher of iced Joe on hand to cool 'em off.

Western Ommm-let

One of the turnoffs of getting up for Sunday morning yoga is getting up-close-and-personal with a room full of barefoot strangers. Unless the strangers are your best friends! Call your local yoga studio, or gym, and ask if any instructors are available for a group private. Then invite yogis and newbies alike for a class right on your deck or back lawn. Set the "space" with a couple of happy-look-ing saris on the tables, flowers and a sampling of essential oils to dab. These aromatic mood elevators come in exotic floral scents like jasmine and bergamot and blends with names like Inner Child—all with different properties that will get guests mixing and sharing. After the class, once everyone's chi is aligned, they'll be blissed-out enough to appreciate any health munchies you conjure.

A Smoothie Bar: Export the blender, along with a selection of smoothie fix-ings—strawberries, watermelon, pineapple, yogurt, apple juice, OJ, Myoplex. Guests choose their own combos. Instead of coffee, brew a pot o' chai.

Pro-Protein: For more substance, egg-white tortillas are one of those super healthy dishes that can be made in advance, served at room temperature, and sliced up like a quiche or pie. Use whatever's most in season—leek-shrooms-ham; tomato-crab-basil. Serve sunflower bread or a favorite whole-grain. Take the toaster outside, too. Serve with butter and honey.

Tunes: Instead of tinkling new age music, download some basement banghra—Indian club music—to keep the energy flowing.

Thelma and Louise Getaway—Road Food

The ultimate on-the-go brunch is actually going somewhere. Set out on the open road for a day trip to visit one of those spots you saw on your View-Master as a kid, or some tourist destination you've always put off. Make a party of the journey. As hostess, stock the car with pillows and snuggly throws, eye shades and other amenities purloined from your last Business Class flight. Organize some *Thelma and Louise* sounds. Speaking of fugitive femmes, the less road-side stopping the better. Bring your own fast-food breakfasts. Everyone gets a brown bag with their name on it, like you used to on field trips in the yellow bus. Inside, pack Wafflewiches: two Eggo waffles filled with bacon slices, a drizzle of syrup and possibly a scrambled egg. Wrap 'em in aluminum foil to keep warm. Add a juice box, and some snack fruit, or fruit roll-ups. A thermos full of café con leche should help beat the traffic. Fill the glove compartment with anti-boredom supplies and treats: Twizzlers, Tootsie Pops, bubble gum, a harmonica, a Polaroid camera for keeping an instant souvenir album, Jack Kerouac's *On the Road* on CD. You may never come home.

Good Morning...
We're Still Here!

Weekend guests are the true test of hostess stamina. Forty-eight hours of straight entertaining. Imagine what it was like in Edith Wharton's time, when it was common to invite guests to stay not just weekends but *weeks* on end. Back then hostesses had a more laissez-faire approach. They set up the invitees in style with a servant to tend the fire and polish their riding boots, but after that it was incumbent on the guests to do some entertaining, too. Good ones brought bright bits of gossip, shared a facility with the piano or were a desirable partner at the bridge or whist table. Assuming you don't have servants or any idea how to play whist, it's still a good philosophy to provide a few luxuries and after that relax and let guests fend for themselves a bit. Small touches, like they have at your favorite hotel, will make a guest comfy and happy. Big ones work, too.

Give Them a Sign: It's just human nature for even the most welcome guests arriving at your doorstep to succumb to insecure feelings that maybe they're imposing. Persuade them that they're wanted. Make an event of their arrival with a Welcome sign—in the car window when you pick them up at the train station, written in chalk in the driveway, on their bathroom mirror, spelled out in alphabet magnets on the fridge, or just a nice handwritten note on the pillowcase.

Stock the Place with 4-Star Amenities: The room'll be so nice they'll never come out. The drill begins with the bedside table: water pitcher and glass, flowers, mint chocolates on the pillows. To go a step further, stock a minibar.

A baby fridge is a cool thing to put in a guest bedroom, but you could also appropriate a dresser drawer filled with mini bottles, cashews, Toblerone, water bottles, wine and a couple of glasses. An ice bucket somewhere would be handy.

A Little Night Music: Leave a boom box on the dresser with some CDs, or a custom-loaded iPod.

Brochures on the Dresser: Call the chamber of commerce or visit your own local tourist board and pick up info on the attractions in your area. This can encourage guests to strike out on their own, suggest stuff they'd like to do, and take some of the guesswork out of your Julie the Cruise Director role.

Dream Journal: Keep a blank book with pen and sketch pencils on the night table for guests to record their night reveries in either pictures or words. Reading and analyzing the bizarre dreams of previous guests is a lot more fun than seeing the average "Had a great time" in a guest book. Put out *Zolar's Encyclopedia and Dictionary of Dreams*, too, for insomniacs.

Mental Junk Food: A stack of bestsellers, because it's always great to come across one you haven't gotten to. Pick out a title you think your guest might like and

Think of a great hotel. Little touches make a guest feel comfy and happy. Big ones work, too.

Improv-vase

Morning is generally not the time you're dying for big urns spilling over with lilies. Flowers in the A.M. are generally for breakfast trays or a guest's night table, when tiny arrangements in bud vases are most useful. If only you could find one. Don't burn the toast looking for the perfect Baccarat vessel. Plenty of other receptacles will do in a pinch. A champagne flute or that gilded Moroccan drinking glass. A dimpled Orangina bottle. A perfume bottle from your lapsed collection. A silver flask. If the opening of your improv-vase is wide, cut the stems real short. When the neck is narrow, use taller flowers—standard proportion is two-thirds vase, one-third stem.

inscribe it so they know it's theirs to take home. Or lay out a vintage title found at a yard sale, like *Coffee Tea or Me*, the 1960s stewardess "exposé."

Some Bubbly: Nothing gives guests that four-star feeling like a robe and slippers and fluffy towels. If you travel a lot, leave out a beauty bar of shampoos, lotions and amenities collected from hotels you've stayed at. Or have your own house brand—a bottle of luxury bubbles and matching scented candle from somewhere swell, like Santa Maria Novella. Plus a collection of rubber ducks.

Morning-Afters

For the one guest you never want to leave, nip out while he's sleeping and whip up a breakfast treat. Something that will knock him out but seem absolutely effortless. You want to get back under the covers as soon as possible.

Trying too hard first thing in the morning risks embarrassment as bad as overdoing the mood lights and lingerie the night before.

All you've got to work with is a bag of bread, one egg and a bowl of sketchy berries. No worries. French toast was invented as a remedy for salvaging stale baguettes during World War something. As the toast sautés, slice strawberries and cherries into the buttery pan around the toast and let melt. Sprinkle with sugar. If you can still hear wood being sawed in the bedroom, there's time enough to nuke the maple syrup. Find any tray you can cover with white linen. Liven up the OJ with the dregs of last night's champagne and a strawberry on the rim. Alas, yesterday's roses won't stand up. Bad metaphor.

Maple-Leaf Syrup Fondue

Ilene: *One of the exciting benefits of marrying a Canadian is exposure to his homeland's quaint customs, like celebrating their Independence Day on July 1 and calling it Canada Day. Every summer, Rick digs out his box of Canadian party artifacts—napkins with red maple leafs, tiny flag pins, William Shatner records—and invites all the Canucks he can find to drink to their national identity, such as it is, rocking to The Guess Who ("American Wo-man"!), fryin' bacon and sluggin' Molsons into the wee hours.*

After a couple of summers, I jumped off the sidelines and pitched in, turning this beer-fest into a brunch on the roof of our building and finding novel ways to serve his classic national foods. Even better than the Nova Scotia salmon and cream cheese shaped like the maple leaf flag was the Maple Syrup Fondue! Served alongside dippable slices of crispy bacon and pieces of French-Canadian toast. A wondrous breakfast-party concept, because the syrup stays hot so the bacon and toast can be served at room temperature. And no cutlery needed, eh?

Floral Levitra: Remove the petals and sprinkle along the white linen. When the toast is golden, muster all your kindergarten art skills and cut the slices into heart shapes. Transfer the hearts to a plate and spoon the melted red fruits on top. Drizzle with syrup. Very professional. When you hear him call "Sweetheart?" take off your socks, remove the raccoon eyes, dab on lipstick. Too much! Kiss the napkin a few times. "Coooming!"

seize
the day

2

picnics, bbqs,
showers

par-tay diem

That's Latin for "beer in the afternoon." Night parties may be cool, but day parties have heat, if you maximize the sunny sex appeal and fresh-air innocence of organic intoxicants. Cut lawns and cutoffs, strappy sandals, floral-print sundresses that match the garden, mystery-date sunglasses, breezy caftans and wind-chiming earrings, bikini tops and sarongs, ripe fruit, birds and bees, bare skin shimmering while swinging at shuttlecocks or working over the briquettes. With a few Swell strokes, you'll come to appreciate doing it with the lights on.

"Casual" should not equal beer holders and mommy jeans. With a few Swell strokes, suburban style has a sex appeal all its own.

Ski Picnic

The sunset beach party sounds romantic, until the wind picks up, sand fleas descend and it's too dark to see your food. The daytime beach picnic, however, is an underexploited opportunity to feed the Gidget fantasy. To have the whole gang hanging out together flirting in funky bikinis, body surfing, playing nearly nude volleyball, Ultimate Hacky Sack. And because expectations for daytime entertaining are low, it's so much easier to pull off. Serve anything other than a sandy tuna sandwich and you look like a hero.

A Swell picnic shouldn't call for any more food or props than can fit into a top-down party wagon. The last thing you want to do is create formal party fussiness on a beach, so keep in mind the Hostess's Hippocratic Oath: "Do No Harm." Just add a splash to the usual scene: cute food but no cutlery, cocktails but no cups. The main attraction isn't the food or drink, it's the action—some kind of fun or surf game to get the beach bums off their bums. Like waaaater skiiiiing!

Setup: Beach-Blanket Bingo

We picked a ski-friendly stretch of beach where the waves are flat but the bikini tops aren't. And to designate the picnic zone, we laid out the World's Biggest Beach Blanket: overlapped stripes, solids and polka dots into a 20-foot crash blanket using our Swell beach towels, which are round so they never have to be turned to face the sun. We threw some shade—floppy sun hats tossed around the blankets that look good and are there for guests to use if need be. Set up chairs in pairs beneath umbrellas facing the water, like the cabana boys do at the beach club. Designate each hangout with its own cooler of beers or pop and something amusing: a stack of magazines, a plastic pail filled with Goldfish, binoculars for watching the skiiers.

You'll raise the chic factor of the picnic miles by not laying out the food on the ground. We made a surf buffet, a beat-up long board wedged into the bluff. The best part is it floats. Call everyone down to wade into the water for dessert-at-sea.

Nibbles: Sea-Fare

A Swell hostess assumes nobody wants to eat anything heavy or sloppy at a party. That goes double when the guests are in bathing suits. Since this party was late afternoon, we served hearty cocktail-hour snacks rather than an actual meal. Small, portable portions that didn't require cutlery. A menu that could be made in advance, served at room temperature and wouldn't go bad after an hour in the sun.

No mayo and nothing that got soggy. Just simple dishes that tasted like summer by the sea.

Old Bay Shrimp: No beachier mood food. Shrimp doused in this salty-spicy Maryland seasoning mix only takes a minute to cook to a gorgeous coral color and tastes like the best bar food you ever had. Skewering is the only labor-intensive part of the recipe. But it's worth it, because then you can stick the skewered shrimp in a plastic ice bucket filled with sand and pretty shells, and they stand right up like a shrimp bouquet.

Paella on the Half Shell: In Spain, this rice dish filled with seafood and sausage is cooked in an open fire in the sand—their version of a clambake.

We'd once had it that way on a Barcelona beach, and briefly entertained the notion of making paella ourselves before we came to our senses, called one of our excellent local seafood shops and ordered theirs instead. We asked the shop guys to throw in a few dozen clamshells. Before guests arrived, we spooned the store-bought paella from the aluminum pan into the shells, which made easy-to-tote party portions and let us pass the paella off as homemade.

Sips: Watermelon Bomb—The Cocktail That Keeps on Ticking

We have a friend who says, "All you need for a good time at the beach is a watermelon and a tennis ball." It's an even better time if that watermelon is filled with booze. The Watermelon Bomb is an old "recipe" from Cynthia's high school days.

Carve the top off the melon like you're making a jack-o'-lantern, pour in ice, and your choice of alcohol, and churn with a long spoon. Punch a band of holes around the top big enough to stick straws into, then let the melon marinate and the ice melt until it's easy to suck the watermelon "juice" with a straw. Plant the melons on the beach blankets so your fellow sand lizards can lie in a circle and get better acquainted. Sort of like sharing the giant zombie at a tiki lounge.

The only hard part is settling on what to pour in. Vodka, for watermelon 'tinis? Grain alcohol, Cynthia's high school standby? We settled on Bacardi rum, but soon learned the W-bomb is an indestructible party weapon that can tolerate any kind of alcoholic fuel. And can be refilled over and over. We reignited our three melons to take to parties later that night as hostess gifts.

Action: Ski Bunnies

We arranged for a ski boat to meet us at the shore. Guests could wade out a few yards and hop on for a round of skiing and hop off the boat easily and head back to the party. Then even landlubbers who would normally never have committed to a day on a ski boat were willing to jump aboard for a twenty-minute outing. We made sure the boat was stocked with plenty of toys for all levels, from show-offs (a wake board) to spazzes (that blow-up thing anyone can hang on to), and brought our own cushions to dress up the speedboat a touch, and waterproof cameras to capture the spills and thrills.

Grill Liberation

In spite of Title 9 and the ERA, to this day the grill is still a male domain, and many Swell chicks mature to hostess age ignorant of how to work even the basic Weber.

Ever since the earliest cave dwellers were flipping dino-burgers, men have maintained exclusive dominion over meat and fire. Let's remedy that.

A Swell barbecue is a communal affair in which everyone participates: men, women, hosts *and* guests. Not only does this alleviate the pressure to do all that bloody cooking but it also maximizes the opportunity for mingling and flirting over the red-hot coals. So we say the more chefs, the merrier. Especially in goofy aprons, holding a cocktail in one hand, charring dinner with the other. Fire up three or four grills, depending on how many you can beg, borrow or steal, and how many guests you have. A few smokin' scenarios that let everyone in on the act:

Flip Your Own

Kebabs: Whether shish or fish, people will be far more excited about the dish when they get to skewer their own combinations. Set out platters of cubed morsels like chicken, beef, lamb and their accessories—'shrooms, cherry tomatoes, pineapple—then no worries if anyone wants onion or hates peppers. Put out long wooden skewers soaking in water, so they don't burn, and a pot of barbecue sauce with a brush. Present the seafood—shrimp, swordfish, scallops, marinating with lots of fresh herbs—more appetizing than naked raw mollusks. For dessert, more skewers—grilled fruit and prepacked s'mores in tin-foil squares ready to stick in the coals.

Steak Out: One tactical error aspiring BBQ divas make is getting carried away: "We'll just throw everything on the grill!" Guests wind up faced with a plate of charred everything, from zucchini to swordfish, in indistinguishable shades of black. Limit the grillwork to the entrée, particularly when serving something that merits special attention, like a great steak. The more you can get done in advance, the more time to spend partying with guests.

Set a steak-house tone by lining up the picnic tables and covering them with white butcher paper for a tablecloth, held down with some heavyweight table-ware—china plates, silver candlesticks. Write guests' names at their places. Foil-wrap sweet potatoes and ol' Idaho potatoes, and stick them in the oven.

As guests start to arrive, turn it up to 350. Now whip out the martini glasses for gimlets, and circulate. When cocktail hour's done, put the taters on the table, alongside the sour cream and butter. Have everyone sit down to a wedge of iceberg lettuce with Roquefort dressing and crumbled bacon, then trot around the raw sirloins on a platter like they do at any proud steak house. You'll get a sense from the shouts how done everyone likes their meat. While they appetize, flame up the sirloins: a one-inch steak is about three minutes per side for rare, four for medium, five for well. Now sit back down and dig in! Get real good at this and you might consider buying one of those branding tools to sear your signature on the work of art.

A Swell picnic, striving for maximum laid-back style, is a compromise of paper goods and quality hard stuff.

Fresh'n Up Burgers: Sometimes all you really want to serve—and eat—is dogs 'n' burgers but you don't want to come across as chintzy or kitschy. Teach the old dogs new tricks. Like Inside-out Cheeseburgers. Insert a few cubes of cheddar or crumbled blue cheese *inside* a plump patty. The cooked burger's melty center will burst with cheesy goodness on the first bite. With hot dogs, swap plain ones for bigger, spicier bratwurst, served on baguettes or crusty rolls with a riot of condiments—hearty mustards, warm sauerkraut, flavored chutneys. *Und* beer, imported German brew or just cans of old Pabst Blue Ribbon, like they serve with wursts in the Midwest.

Quickie Cocktails on the Half-Shell: Every BBQ doesn't have to be a big-deal meal. Whip out the grill for informal drinks, an end-of-the day stop-by. Serve the easiest appetizer known to man: grilled clams. Buy a whole lot of cherry-stones and little necks—figure about four per person, lay those babies on a medium hot grill and cover. In as long as it takes to open a bottle of Sancerre, the shells will pop open. Done! Drizzle with melted butter and lemon. Really done! Same principle works for oysters and mussels. For more gusto, dress the opened clams with a summery tomato sauce or basil pesto. Plunder the farm stand for more munchies—corn cobs roasted in the coals, tomato wedges served like fruit alongside watermelon slices, with a pair of cute salt and pepper shakers. This is an old-time purist's palate.

Party Armory

When setting up to chow down in the great outdoors, the inclination is to forgo chic for convenience. But there's no reason you can't have both—mix the paper with the good stuff. Invest in a big wicker laundry hamper and stock it like a party trousseau.

Fine Disposables: Flea-market china and mismatched silver can be bought in odd numbers for a song, will look pretty on the table and won't stress you out when they get banged and chipped and have to be tossed. Melamine plates and serving dishes, both vintage and modern in bright patterns like our Swell-brand ones, are pretty much indestructible. Over time, the more patterns and colors you accumulate, the more interesting the table—and the more guests you can serve.

Vintage Tablecloths of All Sizes and Provenance: They can overlap, quilt-style, to cover a long or odd-shaped table.

The Poptail

*Cocktails in the middle of the day sounds sophisticated, but
the truth is, imbibing anything stronger than a beer while the
sun is shining can be—how should we say?—a little rugged for
the average Swell girl? Always looking for ways to blend cocktail hour seamlessly into the rest of our day, we give you the
Poptail, a swell way to do cocktails that is as full of summer
innocence as running after the Good Humor truck. Simply get
hold of a few popsicle molds and mix a batch of fruit juice—
orange and pineapple, guava, pom—with rum or vodka. Go
lighter on the booze than your normal cocktail ratio because
a) it's potent and b) the less alcohol, the easier to freeze. When
the mixture begins to thicken, place popsicle sticks in it and
deep-freeze, overnight at least.*

A Roll of Brown Paper: To unfurl along the picnic table instead of a cloth for that crab-house feel, particularly if you're serving something sloppy, like lobsters. Crayons or markers are always good for random doodles.

Souvenir Place Mats: Ilene buys a pair on every vacation. These kangaroo mats? Our Australian honeymoon. Those Frank Gehrys? From the museum in Bilbao. Good conversation starters, and nothing packs flatter.

Rattan Mats: Spread out on the lawn for a less stiff hang-out zone, with lots of pillows, like those giant beds they have at trendy lounges and resturaunts.

Cushions: Make picnic benches less of a bummer to sit on for long intervals.

A Hefty Bag: At the party, line that wicker hamper with a plastic bag and repurpose it as a cute trash can.

Wheelbarrow Bar

It's so refreshing to see a hostess walking around with a bottle freshening people's glasses. Well, that's a challenge when it means toting a selection of soda cans and beer. A wheelbarrow loaded with ice and bevies is a perfect picnic bar cart. Wheel around the backyard delivering fresh chill bombs to all the boys and girls.

Party Props: Working Up an Appetite

Keep toys on hand for spontaneous games, whether it's an outdoor Ping-Pong table set up permanently like a tennis court, or croquet, badminton or horseshoes. Your gym locker can also hold more informal playthings that are as fun to buy as they are to use. Hula hoops, Frisbees, footballs, water guns, wiffle baseball. If the toys R out, the inner children will play.

Come On, Baby, Light Mine

Gas grills, outdoor oven ranges—for our money, the simple Weber kettle is the unbeatable classic. Easiest to manage, portable and so darned cute! Here are a few 'cue cards.

First step: Open all the dampers, or vents, on the bottom of the kettle and the cover. Remove cover and cooking grill and heap briquettes on the lower grill—in the center for "direct cooking" for dogs, burgers, steaks, anything that requires less than thirty minutes. Light up coals with fluid and a flaming newspaper or electric fire starter—you'll come to know your pyro method of choice. Let briquettes burn until they're covered with a light layer of ash— about twenty-five to thirty minutes. While the coals are heating, "clean" the cooking grill with a wire brush. Once you're done it should be time to spread the coals out evenly, replace the cooking grill and lay your supper on there. If the fire's too hot, partially close the dampers to reduce heat; leave them wide open for the highest heat. The top damper should always be open. A rule of thumb is to leave the lid off while the coals are heating, on when the food is cooking, unless you're searing or browning; then keep the cover off. When you're done, close all dampers and the fire will go out. That simple.

Tailgate Party
in the Front Yard

Even something as all-American as the backyard barbecue can start to feel as old as the ashes at the bottom of your grill—and a new tuna marinade recipe isn't going to do the trick. One way to blow some life into those briquettes is to move the grill, and the shindig, from the backyard to the front. Pull a few cars into the driveway or onto the lawn and set up the party right out of the back of your ride. Merge the BBQ with that other great American outdoor partying experience, the Tailgate.

Invites

On blank bumper stickers we jotted down the where and when in colored markers. You can punch it up with a cute catchphrase or catchy song lyric— "Pull up to my bumper, baby."

Setup: Calling All Cars!

We sent out an APB to friends with SUVs and station wagons (great for serving out of). Because Ilene's front lawn was a disaster anyway, we pulled the cars right up onto the grass, flipped open the trunks and made each vehicle a party station. Cynthia's red 1965 Galaxie 500 convertible became the bar. The trunk of Ilene's '87 Shaguar held the snacks. In the back of an SUV we stacked china plates and rolled-up floral and striped linen napkins in preppy colors like pink, navy and green. A preppy-chic tailgate vibe is a good excuse to mix high and low: silver cocktail shakers and plastic cups, the more mix-matchy the better. Odd family heirlooms are good, too—bring on the dents and chips.

For seating you could use folding chairs and chair pads, like you take to a football game, or box pillows. We dragged some backyard chaise longues to the front and had Hudson Bay blankets for partiers to spread out, picnic-style—and filled a big hamper with knit sweaters, hats and scarves for guests to throw on later that night.

We sent out an APB to friends with SUVs and station wagons. In the backs, we stacked china plates and rolled-up floral and striped linen napkins in preppy colors like pink, navy and green.

Sips: Shakers and Thermoses

The Cooler Bar: A proper bar calls for ice and a surface on which the bartender can work her magic. Our solution was to stack coolers. A tower of three made a bar the right height to put out shakers and fixings for our preppy cocktail of choice, PV&Ts—Pink Vodka Tonics, with a splash of grenadine and green fruit skewers, alternating lime and kiwi.

The Hotter Bar: When the temperature drops and it's dessert time, out with the thermoses of cocoa and an array of wee bottles of amaretto, sambuca, peppermint schnapps—all those airplane liqueurs you never thought you'd drink but are perfect for spiking cocoa. Add marshmallows on cocktail skewers and stir.

Nibbles: Honk When Dinner's Served

For some prepsters cocktail hour is the first meal of the day, so we served "Hot" Deviled Eggs with spicy yolk filling, and Billionaire's Bacon, a supposedly Wasp-y treat enjoyed by blue-blood fashion darling Bill Blass—thick, crisp slices of bacon baked with brown sugar, almost as chewy as beef jerky. Celery chips and smoked salmon spread—more pink and green. All prepared in advance, packed up in Tupperware and served at room temp.

Snack Totes: Guests will be disappointed if you don't have pretzels and chips, but those giant plastic bags look, as Muffy would say, TTFW. We used L.L. Bean bags to carry around the Lays, monogrammed RAH RAH, but any set of initials will do.

Mealwiches: Continuing our philosophy that nobody likes to eat with a knife and fork at a picnic, we did soup and sandwiches with the whole meal between the bread. On the grill we flamed up sirloin tips for steak au poivre sandwiches, dressed with black pepper cream and watercress on French baguette. And a BBQ chicken option with our own "appleslaw," store-bought coleslaw customized with apple and caraway seeds, on sourdough rolls. The soup was shrimp bisque, laced with sherry in floral china teacups.

Dessert: Football Snaps—chocolate or ginger cookies shaped like footballs, with white icing "laces."

Action: Gotta Have Game

A tailgate is a precursor to the big game, so organize one. At least have a pigskin or two for passes out on the street. For those who really just like to watch, show a movie on the side of the house: *Varsity Blues* or *The Longest Yard.* Anything but *Brian's Song.* Our screen was a drop cloth tacked onto the side of the house. After dark, with our rented video projector, we turned the front yard into a drive-in.

Showering Off

Getting married and having a baby are two fairy-tale girly events whose celebrations we have to admit can bring out our rebel Tom-girl. Those estrogen levels are overpowering. But what can you do? Nobody likes a cold shower. Embrace all the ultra-femme froufrou and finger sandwiches. Think of showers as if they were the make-believe tea parties you had with Skipper, Barbie and Mrs. Beasley when you were 10.

Lovey-Dovey Luncheon

Let the wedding be subdued and tasteful, the shower's the chance to be eccentric, colorful, opulently romantic.

Invitations: Mail out a twist-on bird with a scrolled-up invitation attached to the wire that reads: "A little birdie told me . . ." Send a piece of knotted string: "Don't Forget. Save the date."

A Solid Foundation: A simple idea with big visual impact is to make each table a different color story, coordinating linens and flowers and even food to match. The pink table gets pink sweetheart roses, pink grapefruit sorbet, raspberry iced tea and so on. Then you can use simple glass bowls and dishes, which will twinkle prettily with all the color underneath and are easy to rent. And since they're see-through you could lay a few pretty words of poetry or a photo underneath.

Tying-the-knot Napkins: Pieces of rope tied in a fat knot make nice-looking wink-wink napkin rings.

Flower Girls: In lieu of a floral centerpiece, leave a corsage at each place, both the wrist and pin-on kind, with the guest's name on the accompanying card: Place card and favor in one.

Centerpiece: Smallish wedding cakes of the plain variety are a deal at the local Italian bakery. Inscribe each tier, birthday-cake-style, with upcoming vows: "I do"; "I will"; "I do." And do a cute cake topper: two lovebirds or a funny bride and groom.

Think of showers as if they were the make-believe tea parties you had with Skipper, Barbie and Mrs. Beasley when you were 10.

Sweet and Spiked: Make heart-shaped finger sandwiches to accompany the different colored and flavored iced teas. Borrow an old Southern Dame trick for giving the tea party a kick and add a dose of Mama's special medicine—Southern Comfort and sugar syrup.

Another Chance for Romance
Birds and Bees: Find fake bees at a hobby shop and stick them in the flower arrangements; twist little birds on the napkins. Serve white-dove-shaped lovebird

cookies. Play with the lyrics to "Let's Do It (Let's Fall in Love)" by Cole Porter: "Birds do it. Bees do it. Even educated fleas do it. Let's do it, let's fall in love."

Adam and Eve: Place an apple at each place, along with a fig-leafed Ken and Barbie sitting among the plants.

Hollywood Brides: Gather stills from your favorite onscreen wedding scenes— Katharine Hepburn in *The Philadelphia Story*, Barbra Streisand as the pregnant bride in *Funny Lady*, Cameron Diaz in *My Best Friend's Wedding*. Mount one on each table instead of table numbers.

Storytelling Shower: Tell the tale of the couple's romance. Someone clinks a glass and recounts how they met. The next person describes their first date,

"Birds do it. Bees do it. Even educated fleas do it. Let's do it, let's fall in love."

and so on, up to the proposal. It could be very sweet to videotape or just record in a souvenir guest book. The story will be jumbled, with people jumping in with recollections at all points, until the maid of honor, or whoever's in charge, ties things up by raising a glass and offering a toast. "And we all hope they live (now in unison) Happily Ever After!"

Growed-Up Baby Shower

It's tempting to infantilize baby showers with votives in baby bottles, candy pacifier rings, the works. But a little of that goes a long way. Hell, this is the last blast before there's a baby wreaking Fisher-Price havoc on your home. Might as well preserve an element of maturity. And make it daddy-friendly. What with all the "We're pregnant" and stay-at-home dads, he and his friends should be as comfortable at the shower as in the delivery room. That might mean playing down the gift-opening ceremony; oohing and aahing over the Diaper Genie will send even the most metrosexual male into a coma. Pick a classic theme everyone can relate to like bedtime stories.

Nighty-Night Invite: Write the party details in storybook prose. "Once Upon a Time . . . there was a shower for Hillary . . ." Invite guests to bring their favorite kid's book as a gift.

Tiny-Love Touches: Rattles tied on champagne flutes. Put the flatwear in white nappies, pinned with a pink-and-blue safety pin.

Baby's Breath: This FTD filler flower will look sweet in tiny arrangements with itty-bitty carnations and rosebuds. Use small containers like a porringer (those Victorian cereal bowls with the elaborate handle) or a silver baby cup. It's a good excuse to have your mom find yours.

Baby Food: Now's the perfect time to indulge your fetish for bite-size edibles, from baby carrots and dip to wee cupcakes iced with pink question marks and blue exclamation points.

Past Your Bedtime: Not only do your friends bring a favorite bedtime story but they also read it—on tape. A funny party activity, with guests creating a live studio audience, a great memento for the future mom and dad. Instead of having to read to Junior every night, they can go to the videotape: "This is Aunt Sally and I'm going to read you *Goodnight Moon.*" "This is Uncle Jimmy and I'm gonna read you the racing form."

Ready or Not: Another good game for a co-ed party is a version of the Newlywed Game that tests how prepared the M&D-to-be are for parenthood. The guests come with a question on childrearing. They ask the question out loud. Each prospective parent writes his and her answers on a cardboard square. Dad shows his, and we see if it matches Mom's reply. How long does breast milk last? What temperature sterilizes baby bottles? If your teenager borrows the car without asking and gets into a fender bender he a) is grounded for life, b) pays for it himself, c) needs a good talking to and a hug. This game can also be done by prerecording Dad's answers on video. Then after Mom shows her answers, cut to the tape to see if they're on the same parenting page.

This is the last blast before there's a baby wreaking Fisher-Price havoc on your home. Might as well preserve an element of sophistication.

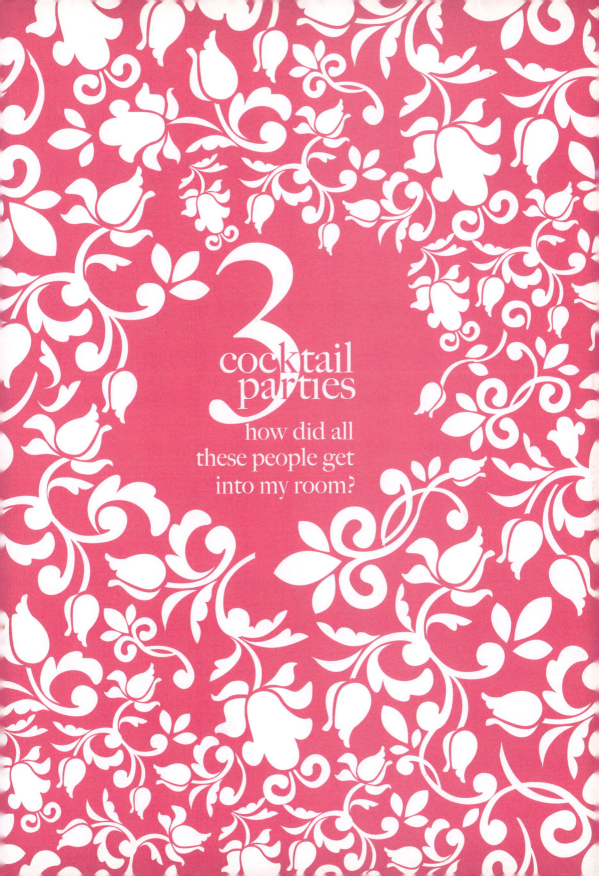

3
cocktail
parties

how did all
these people get
into my room?

managed mayhem

Two jiggers of sophistication and a shot of silliness—the cocktail is the Swellest of all parties designed to shake and stir things up. Its roots date to the Roaring Twenties, when Prohibition spawned underground basement dives that sold whiskey in coffee cups. There were once thirty-two thousand speakeasies in New York, and to make their harsh bootlegged booze go down easier, the entrepreneurial proprietors came up with combinations involving sugary mixers, fruit juices and delinquent names like The Suffering Bastard and Angel's Tit. The cocktail was born in an atmosphere of giddy lawlessness, and so it should remain.

The best cocktail parties are as fizzy and intoxicating as the stuff in the glasses because they swizzle three essential ingredients: alcohol, music and mayhem. The hostess must lubricate her guests with spirits *and* spirit.

What'll make the hour happy is loose lips and flying phone numbers, soft lighting and sharp wit, fashionable looks and second glances, light hooliganism and as many flirtation aids as it takes to loosen stiff guests after a hard day in the cubicle salt mines.

Inviting

In the speakeasy spirit, keep the guest list fast and loose. Anyone goes, as long as they're not a fink. It's not like a dinner party, where you have to worry about matching political views or excluding so-and-so's ex. Clashing personalities make more noise, and who wants to hear their own dumb small talk? The best cocktail parties foment surprise encounters, a fascinating conversation with someone you just met. Or spotting someone you haven't seen in *years*—and then hiding behind a palm tree!

There are a few things to bear in mind. The boy-girl ratio should be as even as possible. If the scales are going to tip, tip toward the guys. Not just because we like the odds to be in our favor but because men are more practiced at amusing themselves in same-sex drinking situations. However, if the ratio is too stacked, they'll complain they're at a "sausage factory."

The party doesn't have to be big. The intimate cocktail—inviting a dozen friends for a quick drink before going to dinner, a show, or solving a murder (like in those old Thin Man films)—is a lost art ready to be revived. For a small scene, a phone call or an evite is fine. But if you're going to the effort of gathering more than, say, twenty, do your party justice and mail out invitations. They get people excited. While you're at it, print a few extras to carry around. You'll be more inclined to make a bold move and pass out a spontaneous invitation to someone you find intriguing and would like to get to know better.

Envelope Stuffing: To Set the Tone, Do Your Own

- A cocktail napkin scribbled with the coordinates.
- A coaster on which you write "Come 'Round for Cocktails."
- A quick hello on a personalized note card, a postcard, or vintage stationery.
- Balloon with a note telling them when to show up for their breathalizer test.
- A feather: "We'd be tickled to have you."
- Tarot card: "Your future holds a Swell time on Sunday night."
- Matchbook with your address on the inside and a note that beckons, "Let's Get Lit."

Party Armory

Not all cocktail parties require formal invitations. They lend themselves to the impromptu if you follow the Girl Scout motto: Be prepared. Have the necessary supplies on hand and you'll find yourself yielding to the last-minute impulse to say, "Let's go back to my place!"

Streamline the Bar

The easiest, Swellest strategy is to have one (at most two) specialty cocktails up your sleeve and the minimum booze and mixers to meet special requests. Unlike dinner guests with neurotic food requirements, entrenched drinking habits are to be indulged, because they often belong to the life-of-the-party characters you want to keep happy. To be safe, always have on hand:

- Something white: Vodka or gin—in the freezer.
- Something brown: Bourbon, whiskey or Scotch.
- A six-pack of imported beer; Bud drinkers will drink anything.
- Club soda and tonic.
- White wine, because they're fussier than red wine drinkers.
- Champagne, then there's always something to celebrate.
- Citrus. Generally lemon and lime wedges are fine, but never put anything with pulp in Scotch or a 'tini. Just a twist, that long strip of peel you sink into a drink.

Make Mine Neat—Accessorizing

Every Swell hostess has a bar. Designate a cabinet, a cart or just a shelf, but choose a spot in the house where you store your barware and party supplies, giving them the same due as you would your beauty products. Equipment is key to styling your cocktail functions. The right supplies separate the girls from the women. One way to develop your own bar style is to adopt an icon. Every time you come across a vintage rooster shaker (cock-tails, anyone?), a sexy-kitten matchbook or glasses emblazoned with your signature stripes, you'll have to have it.

Jigger: The 1 1/2 oz shot glass takes the guesswork out of measuring liquor. It guarantees more consistent praise for your mixology, particularly when you're trying new recipes.

Glasses: Few of us have enough space or dedication to the cause to acquire all the highball and lowball glasses and tumblers and stems and flutes that cover the world of drinks. As with imbibing, don't mix white and brown: the lowball

Dress Codes: A Swell invitation is never bossy. No ordering what to wear; that's a sure way to start people calling and asking for wardrobe advice. Just include a few teasers about the festivities—"Come offer champagne wishes and caviar dreams to Stephanie and Tad by the Von Fussenbergs' pool" or "Join our first annual pig roast and baton twirling"—so people can decide for themselves how they'd like to dress. Head-to-toe plaid would probably work at both.

The easiest, Swellest strategy is to have one (at most two) specialty cocktails up your sleeve and the minimum of booze and mixers to meet special requests.

glass is perfect for anything on the rocks—neat Scotch drinks and even wine can be sipped from a lowball glass (as they do in Rome). But no martini or gimlet drinker will enjoy her drink in a lowball. For stemware, add a set of martini glasses, good for all chilled drinks. Hence the stem, so the drink doesn't get warm in your 98.6° palm.

Pitcher: Necessary for all drinks that are stirred, not shaken. Be sure to have a long stirrer. Nothing worse than dragging out a wooden spoon to mix mojitos.

Shaker: Pull that underloved dust collector out from the back of the shelf. People think they're only for martinis, but familiarize yourself with the shaker and it'll prove a true friend. Shaking—and thus blending, smoothing, thoroughly chilling—makes almost any drink taste better. It's especially useful if you're caught by surprise with only bar dregs to work with—rum, lime juice, ice. Shake, shake, shake. Now you've got a round of daiquiris.

Muddler: Excessive? Nah. This rounded wooden masher is a handy device for making drinks as old fashioned as an old-fashioned and any of the new age concoctions, like lychees muddled into a saketini.

Tray: To serve and collect empties, two work together like an in-out box. Silver, like black, goes with everything. Vintage sixties plastic trays are affordable collectibles. Find one you love enough to leave out for storing your bottles and barware full-time.

Ice Bucket: And a scoop or big silver spoon. A class bartender has a small bowl or bucket for the rocks that go in your glass while she keeps the bottles and cans chilling on separate ice.

Cocktail Compass

There's a logic to why some cocktails just seem to go down better at different times of the year.

Summer—You need ice (rocks or crushed) to stand up to the heat.
White liquors: Mixed with anything fizzy and refreshing—vodka tonics, gin & Fresca. Save the stronger straight-up varieties ('tinis, gimlets) for colder weather.
Dark liquors from hot climates: Rum! For daiquiris, coladas, mojitos.

Fall—Keep it smooth, chilled, straight up.
Drinks with winter citrus: Greyhounds, screwdrivers, salty dogs, Harvey Wallbangers and cranberries cape codder, cosmos.
Cool-weather martinis: From lychee to chocolatee to applee.
A Manhattan: Or anything whiskey-based that should be drunk in a trench coat on a rainy night.

Winter—When the weather's freezing a cocktail should warm you up.
Champagne cocktails: (Spilling over from New Year's to Valentine's).
Liquor from cold climates: Scotch (from Scotland), single malts or Dewars with a twist.
Vodka: And nothing, or dressed up as a Black Russian.
Cognacs, brandies, toddies: Libations that give you a fiery glow.

Spring—Zippy beverages with some herbal zing!
Pimms' cup: Pimms #1, ginger ale and cucumber.
Americano: Campari with sweet vermouth, soda and an orange twist.
Mint juleps: While this bourbon-based drink is a southern summer specialty, now it's associated with the Kentucky Derby and spring.
Margarita: Very spring break.

Drinks Stirrers: Make much of your penchant for collecting, then guests will soon bring them as hostess gifts.

Coasters: Not every glass needs one. Just throw down a few to protect certain furniture—glass, wood, marble—from smudges and rings. They're so small you can have a variety: colored cardboard, cork, cane, crocheted. Improvise with big leaves, or Polaroid coasters with photos. On the bottom you write COASTER.

Napkins: Hopefully you have more friends than cloth cocktail napkins. For those occasions when you expect a full house, paper is more realistic. You won't sacrifice high style if you invest in printing a box with a personalized insignia, like those made for weddings or bat mitzvahs, only these versions last longer than one night. A butterfly, a fox, your address, 21 Lounge, a made-up name: Kit's Club. Monogram initials or a word—FUN or LUV. Or just buy a variety of solid-colored napkins and stack them into a stripe.

Garnish Bowls: You need these for lemon twists, olives and cherries. A trio of odd but pretty glasses can do, too.

Getting Fruity: Invest in an electric juicer or blender.

Corkscrew, Bottle Opener: Yeah, yeah, and don't forget to tie your shoelaces.

Cocktail Berlitz

- Build: Pour ingredients right into the glass.

- Neat: A single alcohol that is served with no ice, and not mixed, as in Scotch.

- Straight Up: A mixed drink served without rocks.

- Float: A tiny amount of liquor poured on top of a cocktail.

- Dry: The more gin or vodka (and less vermouth), the drier the martini.

- Aperitif: Before dinner.

- Digestif: After dinner.

. . . Good night.

Hey, Bartender

Familiarize yourself with the more refined and delicate matters of the 'tender art.

- Serve drinks as far away from the food as possible; it's good for circulation.
- "Box" the bar table with a cloth to hide anything stored underneath it.
- Set up the bar in order of use: glasses (upside down) at one end, then ice, booze, mixers, garnish stirrers, napkins.
- Carbonated drinks shouldn't be stirred: they go flat quicker. Don't shake them either.
- When garnishing, pierce the fruit or olive with a toothpick or stirrer. It looks nicer and is easier on the hungry guest.
- Take the snowy look off ice cubes by sprinkling them with lukewarm water.
- To frost a glass, wet the rim with a slice of lemon or lime, then dip in sugar. Pour cocktail to just below sugar line. Looks even better in a pre-chilled glass.
- An egg white, when shaken with other ingredients, gives a clear drink, like a pisco sour, a white, smooth look and frothy head.
- Don't forget to mix—with the guests. Make the first round of drinks, then suggest everyone refill their own.

Hostess Magic

You cannot make or break the party, but it's amazing how much influence a hostess can have on the mood in the room.

Whenever possible, greet new arrivals rather than waiting for them to find you. How good would you feel walking into a room and seeing the hostess throw her arms up in the air and announce to the world, "Jenny, at last! Now the party begins!" Your mood is instantly ramped up, your status as a valued guest asserted. Fuel that confidence with liquor and wreck some marriages.

When standing in a group and a new person tentatively shows up, stop talking. Few stories are that good. Give a big hello and introduction, and in ten words or less catch them up: "We were just talking about this veterinary psychologist I met . . ." If you were just at the punch line and don't want to stop, put your arm around the guest or take hold of her in some way while you finish so she doesn't have that awkward I-got-here-at-the-wrong-time feeling.

Don't forget to ask, "How's your glass?" The mark of a great host is remembering what your guests drink. Also their names.

Loose and nutty is good. But don't get too tight. It's unsettling for guests, like seeing your mother drunk.

Get around. Sling a camera around your neck, tote a magnum of champagne to offer free refills. If you spot a bored guest, never ever ask, "Are you okay?" Use euphemisms. "Can I get you something?" "Met anyone interesting yet?"

Cause trouble. Sleuth. Pass notes. Whisper secrets. Make introductions from afar. "The guy in the argyle sweater keeps staring at you. He has a yacht docked in Palm Beach." Break up cliques. Ask one of the Heathers to help change the music. Rescue guests from monologuists. Don't get stuck in an entrenched circle. You can always break away with a simple "Excuse me. Be back as soon as I can."

Haute-ess Couture

It's exciting for guests to see a glam host. But a whole sequin dress, long gloves and pumps is going to look like retro overkill. Sexy is good, but you may be taking trash out in the middle of the party, so keep it real.

Temper the Flash: Go for the sequin shell or plunging sparkle top but chilled out with trousers or jeans. If wearing a hot frock, steer clear of the piled high hair: Do messy hair or a pony instead.

Bada Bling: Big earrings, cocktail rings, bangle bracelets, and bigger-than-life false eyelashes can work to pump up the jeans or a plain black dress. Metallic strappy gold sandals can work as fashion Zoloft, too.

Tame the Boa: Those feathery things have looked dead for years. Revive this fluffy tramp accessory by making it shorter, stole length, and sewing on some bright colored ribbons to the ends, tied in a bow. Or clasped with a fire-y brooch.

Classics

The Little Black Dress of Parties

Smoky nightclubs with bow-tied waiters who know you by name. Men flashing cuff links, slipping crisp fifties to dames for powder-room tip money. In the golden age of cocktail culture, legendary haunts like The Stork Club, El Morocco, and "21" made famous drinks like the Manhattan, sidecar, gimlet, daiquiri. Those times have come and gone, but to recapture that black-and-white glamour, celebrate one of the giants from the time before cosmopolitans ruled the earth. Give some props to the original 'tini, or better yet, to Sean Connery's 007 version:

> "A medium dry martini, lemon peel, shaken, not stirred."
> "Vodka?"
> "Of course."

Though we think of Bond's taste as classic, at the time he was a rebel in a tuxedo. Previously, the standard had been gin—stirred, not shaken.

Push Your Fixings Out on a Portable Bar: Call it the "lunch cart," as Dean Martin did, wheeling one onstage at the Sands. Hang his slogan on it: "Don't Think. Drink."

Decorate Your Drinks Trays: Use a cluster of white carnations, the pinky ring of flowers. Use starched men's white handkerchiefs for cocktail napkins. If you tolerate smoking, serve colored gold-filtered Nat Sherman cigarettes in a small glass or cigarette case with ashtrays and matchbooks collected from all kinds of conversation-starting establishments.

Keep It Cool: In really old movies, you'll notice that martini glasses were smaller than the ones we drink from, ensuring that imbibers never got stuck with a warm last swallow.

Nibbles: Serve more cocktails—but of the fruit and shrimp variety—in martini glasses. Likewise, pass around some olives, nuts and canapés.

Throw Around 'Tini Trivia: Inaugurating the end of Prohibition, FDR mixed the first legal martini in the White House in December, 1933. . . . W. C. Fields kept a cold flask of martinis on his film sets and referred to it as his "pineapple juice," drinking them for breakfast. . . . Who said, "I have to get out of these wet clothes and into a dry martini"? Charles Butterworth, a 1930s' actor, and not, as is often claimed, those credit grabbers of the Algonquin Round Table.

Tropicana

When it comes to warm-evening entertaining, there is life after margaritas and salsa. Send your imagination South of the Border.

Palmy Weather: Wrap palm leaves around the glasses and tie with twine. Add big, colorful straws for almost any drink. Garnish with a flower, a mint sprig or a piece of guarapa (sugar cane) for a stirrer. To transform the squarest silver tray into a tropical one, get big palms from the florist or flower market and cover your trays or table with them.

Lush Life: Garnish the hors d'oeuvres with ripe, seductive fruits—a bunch of mini bananas, a pomegranate or papaya cut open and spilling its seeds, a pineapple top, a pile of coconut shards with a few casually tossed flowers. Use

bigger fruit to make the buffet more sumptuous. Add watermelon, some whole and some cut in jagged shapes or wedges, like a Frida Kahlo still life.

Souvenir Recipe: Bring back a cocktail from your last vacation, or make it a local discovery. Ours is the "Alberto No. 1," a gem we picked up from Adalberto Alonso, the legendary Cuban bartender at New York's late, great La Caravelle, who updated his native mojito with champagne and vodka. It's beloved not only for its divine taste but for its associations with Old Havana.

Everyone's a Comedian!

Get a microphone and some material. Invite friends over for a few laughs for Open Mic Night. Tell them, "No cover. Two-drink minimum. Show starts at 9."

When they arrive, have comic monologues playing on the hi-fi, a mix of new guns and old-timers: Dave Chappelle, Chris Rock, Woody Allen, Jerry Seinfeld, Rodney Dangerfield. Since comedy routines are generally taped live, guests will hear jokes and laughter the minute they walk through the door. Keep a sign-up sheet and pen on a clipboard and reorganize the living room furniture into nightclubbish groups facing the "stage," the cleared area where the performers will live or die.

Since this party is BYOJ—bring your own joke—put out a couple of gag books for the delinquent guests who come unprepared. Have on hand noisemakers, a gong or cymbals to cut off any big bombers.

When ready to start the show, flash the lights on and off. Take the mic and welcome the crowd. If you have a friend who's a real card, ask him or her to emcee. If no such friend exists, be prepared to take on the job yourself. Have some shtick to set the tone. All you really need is a great (or really bad) opening line. "Is this mic on?" "Okay, well, we've got a great show for you here tonight at the Comedy Flop House." This also could be your opportunity to unleash your comedy alter ego. Swear a lot, if you're comfortable working blue. It'll grab the crowd's attention. Give false introductions. "First up, a longtime friend of the Flop House. She just finished three weeks at the Mount Airy Lodge in the Poconos and has the heart-shaped Jacuzzi jet prints on her ass to prove it. Put your hands together for Tina Gittelson."

If Tina starts dying up there, hold up the applause sign so the audience can cheer her on. If that doesn't work, give the high sign to give her the hook. Oh, and don't forget to wear the comedian uniform: sneakers, T-shirt and blazer, possibly a baseball hat. Come on, it's funny.

Garnish Entertainment

In lieu of an activity that requires everyone's undivided attention, arrange for a little side action, a diversion and conversation fodder. A game or someone with a talent to share. Open the classified section of your city magazine and circle Hypnotist, Sumo Wrestler, Singing Lessons, Palmist, Piano Player, Dance Instructor, Magician.

Party Props: Icebreakers

To help guests find more to talk about, or to help them conceal their lack of social dexterity, sometimes all it takes is a few toys and icebreakers on the bar or scattered around the party. They're particularly good for assisting flirts trying to get to the next level, so no whoopy cushions.

- *Pickup lines: Pass in a small bowl on a drinks tray.*
- *Napkins, coasters and wine charms: All offer an opportunity for playfulness. Use mini View-Masters as wine charms. Write messages on paper napkins ("Share the olive"). Scribble cocktail trivia on the coasters: "What would you be imbibing if you were drinking mascara?" Wine produced in Mascara, a region of Algeria known for the country's best reds.*
- *Barrel of monkeys: Guests become riveted trying to make the monkey chain. Must be some primal primate urge.*
- *Pickup sticks: In a pinch, they also make good olive skewers.*
- *Magic eight ball: Try again later.*

Midsummer Movie Night

Rent a projector and invite friends over for twilight drinks and movies under the stars.

Seating

Lay out movers' blankets—the quilted ones for packing furniture—and brightly colored pillows. Ring the blanket zone with VIP aluminum sand chairs and loungers. Keep extra blankets in reserve for when the sun goes down.

Nibbles: Concession Stand!

Set up a table with stacks of Milk Duds, SnoCaps, Raisinets, Sour Patch Kids, Twizzlers; Compared to the jumbo theater portions, normal-size boxes will look adorably diminutive. Popcorn, of course. The cardboard buckets they sell for mixing paint at the hardware store make great jumbo popcorn containers. Set out a row of toppings, nacho to toffee flavors. For more substantial junk food, do up hot dogs in buns. To keep them warm, slip them into those thermal aluminum sleeves they have at the ballgame, which you can buy online. At the condiment station, decant relishes and chutneys into small dishes alongside the ketchup and mustard. And if anyone eats cheese dogs, put out the fondu pot for hot cheddar sauce with jalapenos.

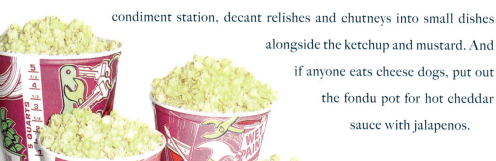

Dessert (because no one's had enough sugar yet): Old-fashioned movie ice cream. Pile the chocolate-covered bonbons alongside Klondike bars still in their pretty foil wrappers (and berries for health nuts) on a tray with handles for the hostess to tote cigarette-girl style.

Preview: Show old cartoons or home movies while guests mill around before the main feature.

The Show

Rent a projector and screen from a video supply company, an easy yellow pages project. It hooks up to your VCR or DVD player, so you'll have to invest in an extension cord to bring the player outside. A screen with its own stand will nestle by the trees or anywhere on your property. Just as good is mounting your own screen on the side of the house with canvas sheeting, thumbtacks and a hammer.

G-rated Sips

Fill a galvanized bucket, a cooler or the Swell wheelbarrow bar with ice and bottles of vintage sodas—black cherry, cream, root beer—they can be spiked with ice cream and vanilla rum for an NC-17 Float.

It's a Mod, Mod World

Mini Makeover

Even just flipping through a fashion mag and noticing that miniskirts are coming around again could be ample motive for a drinks party, one with a mini-Mod spin. After all, the Mod sixties, when miniskirts were invented, were the ultimate swinging party scene. The actual Mods were high-octane London hipsters who zipped around on Vespas in super shorty skirts and wild-colored tights—a renegade combo called "The Look," designed by Mary Quant. To get in the Mod mood, start with the skirt. Invite everyone over for a Mini Makeover.

Make a big statement with one high-impact décor item. Even something as simple as daisies, the cheapest, happiest flower in the garden.

Fashion Chop Shop: All the hostess needs is a pair of fabric shears and courage. Guests bring some dowdy maxi-length skirt from seasons past and take turns standing on the tailor chair and getting chopped up to size. Don't bother with sewing the hem. Leaving the edge raw makes the Mod look more now.

His Look: In Modspeak, the Aces, guys on the cutting edge of music and fashion, wore sharp lightweight suits over Fred Perry tennis shirts. The next level of cool, called Tickets, or Numbers, wore a more working-class look, army surplus parkas over their tennis shirts with turned up Levi's and desert boots.

Set-up: Flower Power

Make a big statement with one high-impact décor item. Even something as simple as daisies, the cheapest, happiest flower in the garden. We got dozens from the green market and filled every container possible with them—glasses, vases, buckets—and turned Cynthia's pad into a daisy oasis.

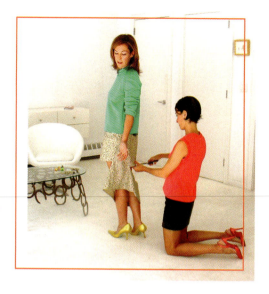

The Look: miniskirts and colored tights. For ours, Cynthia did her instant tailoring trick.

Nibbles

Stick to the pop aesthetic, cool-looking, fast, not too serious. Like pop art, celebrate the iconic brands of the day.

Cheese and Checkers: It's the Squares against the Rounds. Squeeze cheese canapés on Triscuits and Ritzes, served on cardboard checkerboards like game pieces. Jump a cracker and you can eat it.

Ode to Andy: Dress up some delicious Campbell's tomato and serve it back in the mm-mmm-good-looking cans.

Sips—Back to the Future: Tang-tinis

The moon landing was one small step for man, one giant plug for Tang. And it's just as good as apple pucker to shake up with your vodka. We served them on a lazy Susan filled with orange gumballs for extra centrifugal force.

Sounds

If you're tired of your usual tunes, mix in some vintage Mod with Neo-Mod— that is, a playlist of bands whose first word is "The." The Strokes, The Vines, The Who, The Yardbirds (the first super-group: Eric Clapton, Jeff Beck and Jimmy Page, all on guitar), The Stones (back when Brian Jones was still in the band and they all had the same bowlcuts as The Beatles), The Animals, The Turtles, The Kinks, The Monkees.

Food Diplomacy

A buffet table with three cheeses—French, Swiss, Dutch—next to the hummus and pita, beside the salsa and chips, mozzarella balls, chicken satay, jalapeno corncakes . . . Rolaids, anyone? How has the UN approach taken over American cocktail snack policy? You wouldn't eat crazy combinations like that if you sat down to dinner. Why should you just because you're standing up? Simplify. One nationality at a time. Stick to flavors that don't need a translator to go together. And ban anything with garlic, onion or other breath menaces that inhibit your delegates from making close contact.

Adventures in Food Shopping

Every ethnicity has its own brand of junk food. Take the tram to a neighborhood you've been curious about. Then one-stop shop.

Japanese Market: Teeming with crazy rice crackers, shrimp toasts, seaweed-wrapped chips, oddly flavored potato chips. Bags of frozen edamame, shrimp shumai and gyoza dumplings just need to be thawed in a bamboo steamer that you can pick up for a couple of bucks. To splurge, add some sushi rolls. Wash down with Sapporo beer and Satori whiskey, or just serve the sake over ice with a cucumber garnish. (Mix a little Japanese Pizzicato Five.)

Little It'ly: Authentic Italian delis generally sell all the same goodies they serve in Italian cafes at cocktail hour: little bowls of potato chips and olives alongside Campari and soda; those cute amaretto cookies with their fizzy favorite, Prosecco; white beans, anchovies, fancy tuna and other fixings for bruschetta;

bread sticks, dried figs, sliced pepperoni, pepperoncini, bocconcini and some you-got-a-problem-with-that-cini?

Bodega: Let's say you're dying for a margarita party. Foray to the Latino grocery and buy up empanadas, tamales, barbecue-flavored pork rinds, Goya juices.

Pub Grub: If you have a place that caters to English expats, like our favorite NY spot, Tea and Sympathy, you'll find all kinds of "crisps" in flavors like pickled onion, roast beef, chicken tikka masala, Worcestershire and other weird Brit-snacks like Hula Hoops.

Glorified Bar Snacks

Working from your own corner supermarket, you can give basic cocktail fodder a blast of personality.

Warm Nuts: Give a big can of plain nuts a sweet-and-spicy punch-up. In the sauté pan you can fire up chili peanuts, curry cashews, herbalicious mixed nuts in the time it takes to say, "Business Class."

Olive You: Re-dress your favorite kind by draining them, adding your own olive oil and remarinating them with a novel flavor—lemon or orange peel, red pepper flakes on the big green Sicilians, snipped rosemary, thyme, tarragon on the black Moroccans. Wee Niçoises with black peppercorns, lemon, garlic cloves. They last forever.

"Mister" Chips: Even the lowliest Pringle can be gourmet-ified with a flavor sprinkle from your spice rack—paprika, parmesan, garlic powder. Then heat on a baking sheet for a couple minutes. The chips' own oil acts as a cooking agent. Not sure how these store, since there have never been leftovers.

Twisting Pretzels: Raise the bar on pretzels a notch by mixing up the shapes— thins, nuggets, logs, twists served together.   Dips need not be onion-y. Cut the salty with something sweety—honey-mustard dip or chocolate sauce.

Eat Cute

As Steve Martin once said, "Let's get small." Avoid serving anything that you have to bite in half. Cocktail food should be manageable poppables you can finesse with one hand so you never lose your poise or train of thought juggling glasses and plates. Hostesses often think the bite-size hors d'oeuvre is reserved

for passed food, but even at the home cocktail party where you're putting out a few stationary platters, small things will elevate the chic factor. Making them up as you go along is the fun of it. Develop a few of your own classics, and you can whip them out in no time.

Hors d'Oeuvres and Canapés

Grab Your Curly Cocktailpicks—and Stab Away: James Beard, the American culinary lion, championed hors d'oeuvres and canapés as the consummate cocktail food, back in 1940 when cocktail culture was migrating from the nightclub into the living room. An hors d'oeuvre is generally a protein bauble—say a crabcake—served without bread, or as Beard says, "on its own power." Canapés, named after the canopy bed, rest on a bed of toast, cracker or pastry shell. The nostalgic faves are also the simplest, so why not reclaim them, with a few updates.

Hors d'Oeuvres

Shrimp Cocktail: This lovely vintage hors d'oeuvre may seem tired, but you can wake it up by sticking each shrimp with a variety of tasty mates—a vermouth pickled onion, a square of avocado, a slice of smoked salmon. Swap out the cocktail sauce for a trio of new dunkers: a savory sweet chutney mayo; homemade French dressing; a lemony green herb dip. You can do the same with Dungeness crab legs or sliced lobster tails.

Deviled Eggs Recracked: Traditional stuffed eggs have undergone a kitsch craze in recent years, but originally they were laid with all kinds of fillings. Mash yolks laced with anchovy or curry, or make eggs escoffier (ham and gherkins).

Less Crude Crudités: Woeful is the buffet boasting one of those plastic wheels of raw vegetables direct from the supermarket "catering" department. If it's too much trouble to do all that cutting and chopping yourself, serve a single vegetable on a dish or silver platter, mated with a destination dip. Redo stuffed celery by replacing your grandmother's cream cheese and pimento filling with a crab dip or salmon and horseradish cream. Or do something as plain and good as radishes with sweet butter.

Cheese Bored: Who wants to wrestle with a wheel of Brie with everyone looking? Skewer a chunk of cheese with a piece of ham or fruit. Put out a platter of baby cheese balls.

Canapés

Toast: A firm bread like pumpernickel or whole-grain will last longest. If you're making your own canapés, slice into shapes you like—diamonds (the classic), circles, hearts—with a cookie cutter or sharp knife, then toast briefly on a cookie sheet.

Toppings: You could go whole-hog, using a pastry tube to make elegant squiggles, or just hit the same gourmet counter where you'd buy the cheese and pâté for your usual party drill. But instead of serving whole slabs, spread the cheese pâté on your toasts, adding morsels and garnishes that whet your appetite and look good: salmon mousse with a slip of salmon topped with red caviar; white bean spread and good Italian tuna. Mix savory with sweet: Roquefort spread

and a grape sliver, foie gras garnished with Brazil nuts. Hot canapés are as easy as turning on your broiler. Start simple—asparagus tips and prosciutto, melted mozzarella topped with anchovy. Just wait, soon you'll be diving into the crabmeat and Mornay sauce. Stiffen cold canapés by putting them in the fridge for a couple of hours before serving. This allows enough time to make yourself just as appetizing.

4

burn, baby, burn

dinner parties

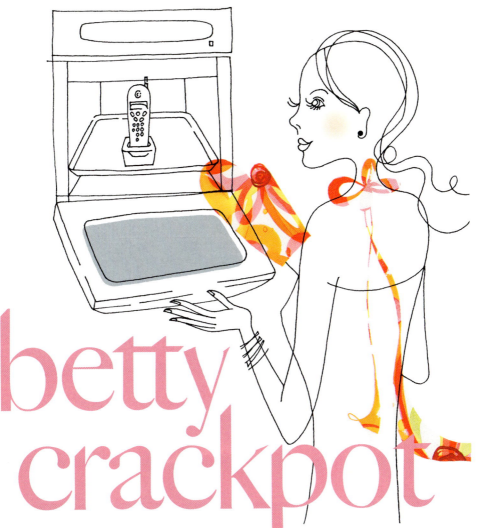

betty crackpot

Not being a chef is no reason not to throw a   dinner party. Of the many

recipes for a delicious night, only one of them calls for knocking people out

with your fantastic cooking: What counts more than the perfect sauce béar-

naise is an appetizing atmosphere that gives people a reason to want to dine

somewhere other than al-Tivo. For a Swell hostess, the bill of fare also includes

spicy company and conversation, surprises on the plate and under it, aphro-

disiacal seating plans. The best dinner party might be one where people are

having such a good time that they forget to eat altogether.

No-Time-for-Dinner Party

One of the cornerstones of Swell entertaining is to eradicate the shame in takeout by tweaking a store-bought menu. This party, however, took the Swell art of self-catering to a whole new level. Rather than disguise the takeout, we celebrated it and made an event of every delivery. Today, you can have pretty much any kind of food overnighted or ordered in, so we arranged for a mix of cuisines, flown-in treats and local specialties, making an exception to our usual policy against culinary commingling (as Emerson sorta said, "Consistency is the hobgoblin of little minds"). At each ring of the doorbell, the guests could get excited over the next mystery arrival. We pulled off an entire seven-course meal, the most elaborate we'll probably ever serve without lifting a finger, except to speed-dial.

Setup

For fourteen guests, one long table lent an air of formality to help dress up the takeout. We rented two five-foot tables and put them together in the middle of the apartment, turning it into a dining room. For a quickie-chic tablecloth, we rolled out some poppy floral print fabric, cut the end and left the hem raw. Cynthia snipped the extra material into napkin squares in the time it took Ilene to lay out her "impatient centerpiece"—impatiens in the same red, pink, white and violet of the fabric, still in their nursery flats, when they always look so lush and full—planted along the center of the table like a runner. Gardening guests could take them home as favors.

Ding-Dong Menu

The air was thick with anticipation—one might say raw nerves—when seven o'clock struck and there was not a stitch of food in the house. But just as the first guests trickled in, the UPS guy showed up with a big box of boiled peanuts from the famous Lee Brothers (Matt and Ted) from Charleston, South Carolina. Now at least there were nibbles while we whipped up a round of blackberry juleps, the only thing we actually made all night. One of our favorite New York bartenders, Dale DeGroff, faxed in the recipe. Not cooking gave us the time to indulge his elaborate concoction, muddling berries and acting like Tom Cruise in *Cocktail*. Good times, until Ilene garnished the last glass with mint sprigs, took a sip and did a spit take. *"Salt!"* Cynthia had accidentally used it instead of sugar.

Beverage recall. We rinsed the berries and started over when the doorbell rang again. The dude in the bowler hat was from a Long Island fish farm that ships seafood. We'd ordered up a raw bar and convinced the hat man to come shuck his oysters in person. When the Chinese delivery boy showed up with the tong shui—sweet and savory fruit-based soups, like chestnut and tapioca pearl with coconut milk—it was time to sit down. Then the doorbell *really* started ringing.

Mad Cow Mania

Conventional wisdom says never test a new recipe on guests. Hah. I live for the anticipatory adrenaline of an uncharted first course, and, in fact, I often find inspiration for a dinner party from the discovery of a new cookbook. Like when I found a deck of French recipe cards from the sixties with a psychedelic pattern on the backs and fifty-two classic dishes on the fronts. Coquilles St. Jacques. Filet of Sole Veronique. Pears Belle Hélène. Pick a card, any card.

I picked boeuf Bourguignon. Essentially a gourmet beef stew from a region of France famous for two things—Charolais beef and Burgundy wine—it's also a mighty dish for a winter dinner with lots of healthy garçons in attendance. The problem was that in the sixties, hostesses had all day to flirt with the butcher, cook and sit under the hair dryer. With four hours of cooking time plus shopping, I'd have to take a sick day to get dinner on the table for guests at eight o'clock.

Rather than fold my cards, I schemed to shop and cook the night before and let the stew "rest" for a day. By the time I finished shopping, I was frying beef at ten o'clock at night—in lard, mind you. I'd have to cook while I slept. So I put the stew on at midnight, set the alarm for 3 A.M., got up, stirred, set the alarm again for 5 A.M. and turned off the burner. After work, all I had to do was make my carottes à la Vichy (glazed carrots—another recipe card), turn the burner on under the boeuf and get to the florist for lilacs to mask any vestige of eau de lard.

Sirloins from The Old Homestead, an old-time New York steak house known for giant portions. We turned them into steak frites with fries from Le McDonald's.

At the peak of the party, Mr. Bowler was sitting at the table, listening with rapt attention to the spiel of

The Mr. Softee truck! We duked the ice cream man twenty dollars to stop by after hours for dessert.

a young, dandyish sommelier we'd befriended, who'd arrived with a tie knot as big as his fist and a few bottles from his secret stash to pour with the cheese course, wheeled over from the restaurant across the street right on the cheese cart.

As the guests were falling woozy with red meat and vino, the bell rang once again. The Mr. Softee truck! Earlier that afternoon, Ilene had duked the ice cream man twenty dollars to stop by after hours for dessert. Everyone grabbed the envelope tucked under his or her plate stuffed with a couple of dollar bills, then ran downstairs. "I thought those were for a stripper," said Tad, one of our pals, clasping his singles. But he seemed glad it was Mr. Softee instead.

Le Menu

One-Dish Wonders

The secret to smooth chef-ing is in the menu planning: something with wow-factor that doesn't imprison you in the kitchen when your guests are already in the living room. Let all the blood, sweat and tears happen before anyone shows up. Avoid anything that requires last-minute stove work. Keep the number of dishes to a minimum. No matter how "easy" the dish, the more you're serving, the busier you'll be with last-minute details and timing and all that harrying stuff. A Swell solution to keeping your Suzy Homemaker polish is to create a whole self-contained meal, one of those miracle dishes that come in a casserole, a roasting pan, or a big pot on the stove and call for no side dish other than salad and bread. Every nation has one.

A Swell solution to keeping your Suzy Homemaker polish is to plan a whole self-contained meal in one big casserole.

Bouillabaise, a fish soup in a zesty, tomatoey broth comes from Marseilles and is traditionally made with a netful of fish from the Mediterranean, shellfish to sea bass. You can buy anything fresh that catches your eye at the fish counter. Present the stew in a terrine and serve with crusty French baguettes and rouille, the spicy spread traditionally served with the fish dish.

Choucroute garni is an Alsatian staple at French bistros. Sauerkraut sweetened with onion and bacon is served with a variety of sausage and boiled potatoes in a big covered casserole. Serve with a *wunderbar* centerpiece, a tureen filled with ice and the best German beers you can find. Offer soft pretzels for bread, like they do at restaurants in Berlin.

In the movie *Big Night* with Stanley Tucci, the climactic dish was the Timpano, a giant pasta casserole with a week's worth of food in it: sausages and mushrooms and baby meatballs and hard-boiled eggs. Approach your "big night" lasagna in the same way and it'll obliterate the need for any second act, or course.

Boozy Starters . . . and Woozy Desserts

Some parties manage to maintain that cocktail-hour buzz right through dinner. If only you could bottle it. You can. To keep the party going past the pudding, aperitifs and after-dinner liqueurs can be the magic ingredients that turn a basic first course into an eyebrow-raiser and a humble dessert into a pick-me-up. Choose one or the other, not all of the below. Temperance is a virtue.

Gazpach-olé: The host walks around with an iced bottle of vodka with a spigot spout offering guests a shot right in the chilled soup.

Fruit Cocktail: Put the meaning back into that dish. Marinate melon balls, pineapple fingers and kumquats in a cup of kirsch, cherry liqueur or Sauterne— French dessert wine. Serve in a martini glass. People won't be late for their fruit cup again!

A Shot in the Dark: How much fun to find a shot glass on your appetizer dish—aquavit to accompany the gravlax, a flavored vodka beside a dollop of caviar on a blini pancake, a hollowed-out lemon half with Mexican Sauza next to the ceviche.

Champagne Sorbet: This is a great dessert or "intermezzo" palate cleanser between courses. If you own an ice cream maker you can make your own. Once you get going you can expand to a medley—mimosa flavor and kir royale sorbet, and so forth. You can also buy flavors like cosmopolitan made with actual cocktail ingredients from gelato companies like Ciaobella.

Strawberries Romanoff: A retro-chic staple. Pour curaçao or Grand Marnier over berries, let stand for thirty minutes, garnish with whipped cream and candied violets. An alternative to marinating fruit is whipping the cream with a few tablespoons of your favorite liqueur and sugar.

Ooh, and do have virgin versions on hand for non-swillers.

"Comme il faut": Classic French Do's and Don'ts

Go to any apartment in Paris for dinner, and no matter how young the hostess, she will pull it off with amazing competence. Go to three dinners and you'll start to wonder, Who sent out the memo? Parisiennes all seem to follow a hostessing guideline as chic and reliable as an Hermès scarf tied around a cashmere sweater. Here's the memo:

Appetizers: No buckets of guacamole or baba ghanoush overkill. In Paris, a hostess is more likely to put out a tiny bowl of cheesy crackers or olives, as they do in hotel bars. Presumably the philosophy is that the hungrier guests are by the time they get to the table, the more delicious the meal will taste.

Aperitifs: The pre-show show is not about how hot the wings are but what bottle you will open. A nice wine, a champagne—even if it's not a birthday or anniversary.

Entrée: Accompanied by bread. No butter.

Wine: A vestige of traditional sexist culture is that no woman should ever pour her own glass of wine. Which seems like a Gallic excuse for flirting every time a girl's glass is too low and her dining companion is too absorbed by his neighbor's décolletage to notice.

Parisiennes all seem to follow a hostessing guideline as chic and reliable as an Hermès scarf tied around a cashmere sweater.

Salad: Always after the main course. Just green. Butter lettuces. A simple mustard vinaigrette with snipped tarragon.

Cheese: Three or four on a block, each with an individual knife. Probably one goat, one blue, two soft. And on a separate dish, butter. Cut round cheeses like pie slices. The great faux pas is to cut the tip (or "nose," as they say) off a wedge of cheese. It will cause audible gasps.

Fruit: They don't do berries or fruit salad. Simply a bowl of fruit in season: clementines, apricots, little apples. Guests choose a fruit like candy.

Dessert: A cake or tarte or other treat from the patisserie, rarely home-baked. Why compete with the pros?

Coffee: Served in the living room, after dessert, preferably with chocolates and more booze—brandies, ports, eau de vies.

Dressing the Plate

In the event that you're serving plated food, as they say in the restaurant biz, put some thought not just into the taste combos but into the rest of the senses, too.

Use Your Eye: Brown meat with mashed potatoes and mushroom sauce will look dreary no matter how yummy. Throw in some color: Peas and carrots became a classic because they're bright and pleasing. So are roasted beets and sweet potatoes. Guests are likely to remember your fabulous duck à l'orange as much for the crispy skin as for the sight of the tawny bird surrounded by candied orange sauce and white orange blossom flowers.

And Your Nose: At this point, a ring of curly parsley on a plate almost seems kitschy. There are so many other herbs in the produce section these days. But choose wisely—an herb that's compatible with the seasoning of the dish. No rosemary on a piece of salmon already poached in dill. Vegetable leaves are an underexploited and versatile garnish. Carrot tops, for instance, look like parsley's feathery cousin and are subtly flavored enough to top even a delicate piece of fish. Edible flowers and fruits can be pulled into service too, but not randomly. Pansies will look crazy tossed on sauerbraten but gorgeous on a leafy green salad or a lovely white cake.

Squeeze Play: A mustard bottle is the secret tool used by chefs to make sauce squiggles. Definitely try this at home, particularly to glam up a store-bought dessert. Fill up the bottle with, say, a raspberry coulis (blended frozen raspberries, at its simplest) and dress up the nude baby cheesecake. Squirt a coulis bow at the bottom of the plate, a pair of hearts, a scalloped border, a ring of dots (type-A chefs use an eyedropper for that) or that signature restaurant flourish, the horizontal wiggle. It's all in the wrist action.

Accessorizing the Table

Flowers in Camelot

Jackie Kennedy revolutionized White House entertaining by forgoing the traditional U-shaped banquet table in favor of a room full of smaller round ones seating no more than eight or ten. She liked the conviviality of close table settings and parties small enough for people to converse across the room. Simple, natural flower arrangements were her thing, inspired by Flemish still life paintings and aromatic enough to double as natural air fresheners (always important in those days when there was an ashtray at every place).

Lilies, though fragrant, should be avoided indoors because their perfume is so intense that they can aggravate allergies or annoy people. Also those pollen-covered pistils stain your skin or clothes when you have to move them into the other room. Jackie no doubt knew that, because she thought of everything. She had the staff burn the taper candles for ten minutes before dinner, to see if they tilted and so that the wicks would be black, not waxy-white.

Tablecloth Tricks

A Swell hostess is never going to have enough real tablecloths to satisfy all her moods, themes and cuisines. But there's no reason to even try when you can snip and rip yourself a new one for every occasion. At a fabric store you can find patterns for all seasons, in 45-, 54- and 60-inch widths. Measure your table and buy enough fabric to cover the length, allowing an extra yard of overhang on all sides.

In warm weather months, get springy fabrics—Liberty print, gingham or Swiss dot to mix in with big polka dots. In winter, go to the same fabrics you'd put in your wardrobe, from bright silk shantungs to flannel plaids to go with the comfort food. Fabrics can be inspired by the occasion. For a guy's birthday, use classic men's shirting and thrift shop ties to knot around crisp white napkins. On New Year's, put out silver lamé with napkins made out of something pretty and beaded.

To get the same versatility from your real tablecloths, layer. Overlapping round tablecloths can work to cover a long table. Mix patterns, geometric shapes and textures. Mod-ify the Battenburg lace by laying it over a really bright orange or lime green undercloth so it's crisp and graphic.

Napkin Notions

While at the sewing store, load up on ribbons and trim to use for napkin rings: grosgrain, organza, lace, metallics, giant rickrack. Take a napkin square, fold back two opposite corners, then cinch with the ribbon and tie into a full bow.

Place Cards

As much as the Swell M.O. is keeping things loose, we get all proper when it comes to sitting down to the dinner table. There's something nice about that old-fashioned gentilesse of a hostess seating her guests, whether with place cards or by simply directing everyone to their seats. It takes the pressure off the guests at that awkward moment when everyone's standing around the table not sure where to go or whom to commit to. Guests appreciate a hostess who has given some thought to people they might like to meet. And if you do find yourself stuck next to the near-mute tax attorney, you can be flattered that your hostess considers you an interesting enough conversationalist to balance the weak link. To take the formality out of seating assignments, use something other than a plain white card, like a Polaroid of your guest snapped during cocktails. Or embellish the traditional place card by adding a nickname or some icebreaking detail about the guest.

Split Decision: Seating Couples

Opinion is divided on this one in the Swell camp. Cynthia thinks it's ridiculous to break up couples. Ilene believes engaged couples and newlyweds should be seated together because they're miserable when they're apart. Otherwise couples together are a conversational dead zone. Temporary separation is a chance to flirt and spout pearls of wisdom your guy knows you just read in the paper that morning. It's sexier to occasionally catch his eye with a knowing look. Besides, you'll have more to catch up about when you get home.

Do Me a Favor

Favors are becoming an antiquated custom, but take-home trinkets don't have to seem so excessive if you make them do double duty as place cards or wine charms or work as an element of fun at the dinner itself. For instance, a sketch pad with a guest's name written on the cover at his or her place can serve as a place card and intermezzo activity. Diners can sketch each other between courses. If all goes well—who knows—you might end up with nude models before the baked Alaska comes out. Surprise favors can be hidden under the guests' dinner plate, so when it's cleared they find a movie ticket for the next portion of the evening or a Cranium card because that's the game you're going to go play during dessert.

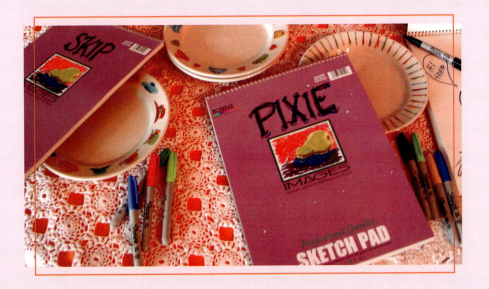

Party favors can do double duty – a sketch pad with a guest's name written on the cover can serve as a favor, place card and intermezzo activity.

Centerpieces

The term *centerpiece* is often incorrectly used as a synonym for flowers. In fact, plenty of pretty, fragrant things can be used for eye candy on the table, many of which will add just as much life to your party as posies. They could be as silly as party hats and noisemakers spilling about, or as opulent as a bacchanalian fruit platter mixed with nuts and candies. We love the idea of a centerpiece you can interact with.

Edible Centerpiece: Looks beautiful and guests can nibble throughout the meal. An icy platter of raw bar treats, a sumptuous crudité installation running down the middle of the table with hollowed-out squashes and artichokes for sauces, all kinds of breads, baguettes, muffins, breadsticks and flavored butters.

Potable Centerpieces: Put wine buckets between each pair of diners with their own bottle to share. This saves you from having to jump up for new bottles throughout the evening, and it makes neighbors into sort of drinking buddies. Filling each other's glasses gives them some friendly business. Pull out the old punch bowl and use it as a giant ice bucket filled with bottles of wine and champagne splits.

Floral Centerpiece: When using flowers, avoid a formal or boring look by appropriating different vessels—pretty china teapots, sterling ice buckets, a confederation of candlesticks. Whatever you use, try to make arrangements below eye level so they won't block guests' views. It's sad to sit down to a table that looks like the hanging gardens of Babylon, then as the first order of business, the hostess removes all the flowers, like clearing away the dessert before you had a bite.

Chat and Chew

Equally important to the chow is the chat. A Swell hostess looks after her guests' conversation as much as she refills their plates.

Come Prepared: If things aren't happening naturally, have a few topics in your pocket that can work as conversational kindling. Tossing out a question to the group is a Swell classic. If it's off the news of the day it'll seem more clever than random. "Have you heard that in the future men will no longer be required for human reproduction..."

Your guests will sing your praises as the consummate hostess if they feel flattered by your attention.

Create Openings: Involve your shy or uninformed guest in the conversation. If it turns to contemporary art and suddenly one of your guests develops the vague, distracted look of an Ozark who lost his banjo, help her out. But not with the question "Have you seen the new Tom Sachs installation?" If she hasn't, she'll clam up worse, and offering a professorial fill-in won't make anyone happy. A party is not the time for a lecture. With your own observation or info tidbit, extend the topic to an area the guest might chime in on. "I hear the new Modernism museum in your hometown, Fort Worth, is sort of controversial. . . ."

The Politics of Inclusion: Make sure conversation doesn't exclude anyone. If the whole table turns to sport, and you spot your metrosexual friend reddening with anxiety, worried that someone might ask his thoughts on the latest Boston trade, change to a safer topic, like sex. That's one thing everyone has in common.

Read the Paper: If it's a choice between going to the florist before work and reading the paper, lose the daffodils. Even if you generally stay current, it's such an asset to have the day's news, movie reviews and new scientific discoveries fresh in your mind when you're trying to jump into the conversation or lead it somewhere new.

Don't Drag out Personal Affairs: Keep it light. No matter if you're still reeling from a blowout with your boss and have vowed to quit tomorrow at 8 A.M., don't vent—compartmentalize. Deep issues and emotions are too much to handle in public even for those who love you.

No Negative Campaigning: The point of dinner party conversation is to have a point of view, but you should express it in an entertaining manner. You don't want to be disingenuous, but expressing rage at the machine for cheating eco-conscious entrepreneurs is boring. Especially if you're the host and people feel they have to listen. Write a letter to your congressman. At the dinner table, hone your Oscar Wilde skills. Wry jokes, witty barbs, even a baiting comment are acceptable. "And I suppose you'll be selling your SUV as a contribution to the environment, Howell" is okay. Yelling, "Only a moron would vote for that fascist!" is not.

Keep It Clean: Your role as host is not stoking tempers but soothing them. When the decibel of disagreement starts making other guests quiet, that's the time to come in with a few referee moves to pull the fighters apart. "Go to your corners." "No hitting below the belt." Hopefully somebody will laugh.

Listen with brilliant intensity: Your guests will think the filet was moist, the candlelight divine, and sing your praises as the consummate hostess if they feel flattered by your attention.

Not-Yet-Moved-In Party

There's always a reason to claim that your place isn't ready for a party. You don't have a proper dining table, you need to paint, all your stuff is still in boxes. Or all of the above, as was the case when we decided to throw a dinner party christening Cynthia's new pad just before she moved in. China, glassware, a working oven? Bourgeois conventions! Indulge the bohemian fantasy that you can live on dreams and love and wine. Especially if it's just for one night.

A sit-down for 20 without a stick of furniture – insane? Well, yes. But on an optimistic note, all that raw space also seemed kind of romantic.

Setup

Cardboard Dining Table: We pushed all the moving boxes into a long free-form banquet table of various heights and sizes. Guests' names were written in fat marker on the boxes at their places. For seating, people lounged on giant orange and pink and gold floor pillows, harem-style. Because the only box we couldn't find was the china, we used brightly colored paper plates, from chargers to

We pushed all the moving boxes into a long free-form banquet table of various heights and sizes.

dessert plates, in pink and orange and gold. As it was February, right around Valentine's Day, we tore pages from steamy romance novels and slipped them under the plates, so when the Vietnamese long noodles, a reputedly lucky dish, was taken away, guests discovered their pages and read aloud to each other about heaving bosoms and aching loins as they helped themselves to champagne splits. Empty paint cans the workers had left behind became tulip vases down the center of our up-and-down table. On the sidewalk, we drew a heart-shaped Swellcome mat in chalk, to mark the entrance of the new love shack.

Wild-Card Guest

Some people think it's embarrassing to ask a person you don't know that well to a party. But if we followed that tack, we never would have invited Rory, a young, rising magician who had the girls mesmerized during cocktails, dazzling them with magic tricks, fire tricks and card tricks, including one that left Cynthia with the ace of clubs stuck on the ceiling. It's still there.

Dinner-Partying Out

Inviting people out to a dinner at a restaurant is an idea associated with a big occasion, a private room, an expense account. That's a shame. A Swell hostess lives for the concept of hostessing with no cooking or cleaning. The restaurant idea is too good to relegate to such rareties. If only there were a way to make it more everyday. There is: do up a dive. People need a reason to slum. Whether it's the amazing stone crabs or the incredible sunset view, a dive has to have some attraction worth writing home about if it's to be deemed jewel-in-the-rough. In the Hamptons, there's this fish farm in the dunes of Napeague. Talk about character. It's like a Steinbeck novel. Rhodesian ridgebacks skulking about and surly geese nipping at customers' heels. In the middle of the mayhem, the two funky broads in charge set up a tiki lounge with picnic tables and colored lights. Perfect.

Setup: Levitate the Table

Stamp your imprint on a public space with your own linens, candles and favors. And since you're not cooking, you might have the time to get all that stuff together. At the fish farm, upgrading was easy because their usual table service involved Styrofoam cups and aluminum serving platters plunked down on beat-up picnic tables. We brought china plates and claw-crackers and gave the kitchen ladies a nice white platter for bringing out the lobsters and lemons. Down the center of the table we tossed colorful firecrackers from Chinatown, farm-stand flowers, striped table candles and a few wee birthday cakes—tacky-traditional ones from the supermarket bakery with icing rosettes in those fantastically fake pinks and blues. A perfect match for the aquatic hues of our fish-pattern tablecloth.

Nibbles: Mrs. Claws

When hostessing out, planning the menu is the extent of your kitchen duties, so enjoy it. Decide on something you like, order it for everyone and don't stress about making the whole world happy. If they were eating at your place, they'd live with whatever you served. Besides, when hostessing, if you order in advance you get better service and fewer screwups. At the fish farm, we went with lobster—at this place they're cheaper than tuna sandwiches—with boiled local corn. Butter on everything.

No cooking means you can afford to give more attention to some of those details you normally might gloss over.

Sips: Home Brew

The fish farm is strictly BYOB. For a summer's eve lobster dinner we might have gone with a well-chilled *fumé blanc* and proper wineglasses for everyone, but to keep the party easy and breezy, we set a limit on shlepping. Instead of carting around nice glasses, we styled up beer bottles. We made our own labels using Cynthia's home brew motto, First Draft: You Have Nothing to Fear but My Beer Itself, and stuck them on the Amstels, accepting all compliments on our pro-quality lager.

Instead of carting around nice glasses, we styled up beer bottles—First Draft: You Have Nothing to Fear but My Beer Itself.

Lady Luck Dinner

When entertaining at a restaurant that actually uses linens and china, bringing your own might seem a tad anal. But there are other ways to stamp your party imprint. We threw a girls-night dinner in LA at Indochine, where the guests included a bunch of young actresses getting started in their careers, so we customized the table with a Lady Luck theme. We covered the table with shiny heads-up pennies and made up a loose centerpiece with flowers interspersed with boxes of Lucky Charms cereal and fortune cookies. Each seat had a place card with a lucky icon—shamrock, horseshoe, ladybug—and beneath each plate was a scratch-off lottery ticket. What good is luck with nothing to use it on? The favors were Cynthia Rowley lip totes in which we'd put a pair of dice for a little action in between courses. Rebecca Gayheart was first to make seven, so she won the grand prize: a parasailing jaunt over the Statue of Liberty on her next trip east.

Tokens of Appreciation

The Almost Generic Gift

On the delightful occasion when you're invited to party at someone *else's* home, a Swell guest is appreciative and shows it with a token that hopefully has a bit more personality than a nameless, faceless bottle of white.

- Cocktail frippery: stirrers, funny coasters, cocktail napkins, novelty ice cube trays, cute picks and a jar of olives.
- A six-pack of champagne splits in a cooler bag.
- A magic trick.
- Nuts and a nutcracker.
- A vintage party book, like something by Dominick Dunne or Truman Capote.
- Insta-guestbook: A small album and your Polaroid.
- Fresh flowers: Mask the origins of deli flowers by rewrapping them in gift wrap, a subway map or winding lots of ribbon up the stems like a bridal bouquet tied in a big bow.
- Outdoor action: Hula hoops tied together, a whole bunch of beach balls, or pool toys that occupy guests trying to blow them up.
- Coffees, teas or an interesting liquor brought back from your last vacation or business trip.
- Good clean fun supplies: a morning-after gift bucket filled with rubber gloves, sponges and aromatherapy cleaning fluids.

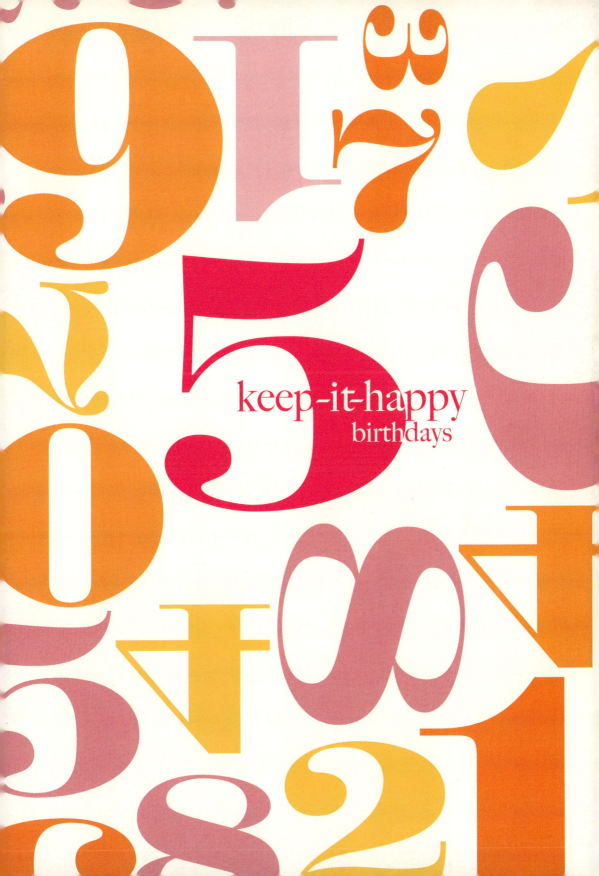

keep-it-happy
birthdays

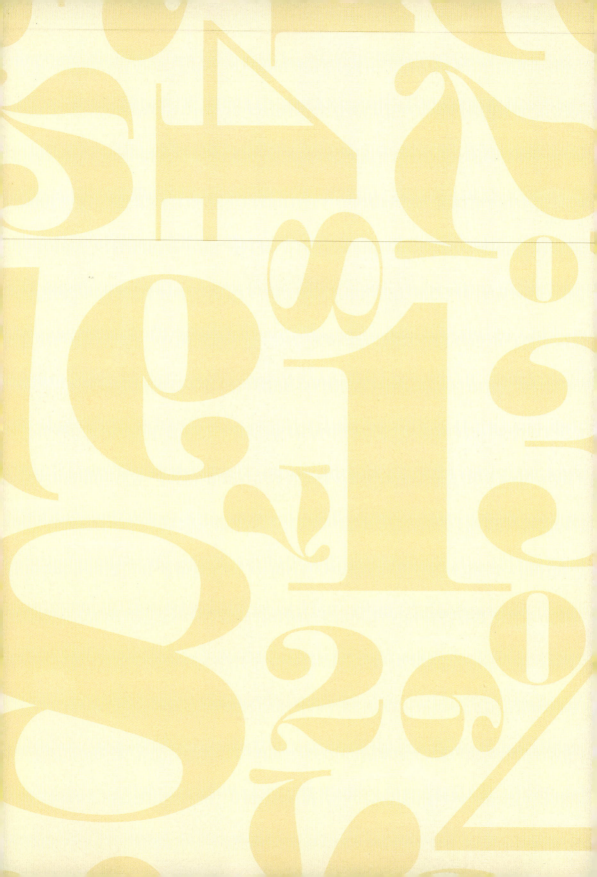

as long as they don't blow

Cake! Singing! A clown sneaking something from Daddy's liquor cabinet! Birthdays walk a fine line between happy! and *depressing*. And not just when you start getting too old for a cake big enough to hold all the candles. Even little kids inevitably cry at theirs. Birthdays raise issues. Who are my friends? Who am I? Why does no one ever remember I *hate* cherry filling! The reason for celebrating is to distract you from all that existential angst. That's why the essence of Swell birthday hostessing lies in your ability to remind the birthday girl or boy of something to live for!

A Thirst for a First

A birthday is an opportunity to plan something to make your heart race with adrenaline, fear, naughtiness, curiosity and make you overtired.

The best way to recapture the youthful exuberance of those earliest birthdays is to experience "a first"—something you never thought you would do or always wanted to try.

This approach doesn't require a mob. With just your honey or a handful of nearest and dearest, you'll still feel like you had a big celebration. A night at the demolition derby. Fencing lessons. A helicopter ride. Bobsledding. Skydiving. The opera—a truly risky outing beacuse it will either be the best birthday of your life or the worst.

Peta Pan Birthdays

Another rejuvenating approach is to revisit one of the classic b-days you had, or wished you'd had, before you hit double digits. Of course, these days, having been around and seen something of the world, you're not as whipped up at the prospect of pizza at the bowling alley. Or are you?

Six Flags Birthday: Rent a minivan, load it with friends and peel out for the amusement park. Everyone gets a party-bag packed with a disposable camera, sunscreen and a hat—a customized baseball cap or paper tiara will make it easier to spot members of the birthday party in the crowds. After handing out the tickets, plan a lunch meeting time and place. End of the day, pile back in the van—devour cake—and sleep all the way home.

Pony Rides: Always wanted a pony at your birthday but never got one? This is your year. Play the ponies to your heart's content, at the track. On the ride out, hand each guest a birthday card with enough cash for a two-dollar bet. Address the cards with their *Guys and Dolls* nicknames: Smilin' Ilene, Harry the Horse, Big Cindy. Also dispense copies of the *Racing Form* to handicap the day's races, and a good luck talisman, like a double-heads-up penny (two pennies glued together). Wear sunglasses and your horseshoe pinky ring. And bring cigars. Even if no one smokes, they'll come in handy when you hit up an old-timer for a good tip. Have in mind a place to go afterward to spend the winnings. If you lose, back to your place.

Day in the Park: Skip the picnic. Play pied piper and lead your friends around like a roving gang of little rascals. Hit the carousel, move on to the petting zoo, rent rowboats or mini racing sailboats. Bring lots of pocket cash for candy apples and chocolate bonnets.

Class Trip: Invite friends for a day of culture to see something new and cool. But don't pack a lunch. It seems every city with a modern museum has now

Birthday with a Catch?

Ilene: *Cynthia's birthday had hit the doldrums—last-minute get-togethers at the local bar—two years in a row. Time for a best-friend intervention. I blindfolded the birthday girl, stuffed her in a cab and took her to the west side of Manhattan, by the Hudson, where a trapeze school had just opened. The rest of the posse was already there, with tutus, tiaras and cake. Cynthia freaked with excitement, always having harbored fantasies of joining the circus. She bounded up the 30-foot ladder and swung out into the air with the greatest of ease. We all took turns swinging by our knees into the night, the city twinkling behind us, until it was time to complete our last lesson—the catch. Birthday girl couldn't pull it off and wasn't going home until she did. Over and over she tried, while the men in tights were getting restless. As midnight approached, Cynthia went a final time, reached out to the instructor, and… grabbed his arms and swung from them, completing her catch. Now we could go to dinner.*

elevated the cafe food service to destination restaurant status with celebrity chefs. So, send a postcard of the Mona Lisa or some inspiring piece of artwork for invitations, see an exhibit that's avant-garde or provocative, and everyone can process the experience in a very intellectual manner over much wine and food in the sculpture garden bistro.

Regression Lounge: Get that kiddy-party rush without leaving home. Make the invite for an adult hour, like ten o'clock, after everyone's already had dinner. Fill the room with streamers and balloons and start the party off with a few rounds of Shirley Temple Blacks—ginger ale, grenadine and a maraschino cherry matured by a dose of Johnny Walker Black. Hire a clown to do balloon-twisting—dachshund, giraffe . . . a different animal for every guest. When it's time for cake, everyone sits down at a table tricked out with paper tiaras, hats, noisemakers, those upside-down ice cream cone clowns. Stacked up in the center of the table: gifts for all the kiddies. A red nose for Timmy, a rainbow wig for Suzy, a clown painting for that girl you don't like. Play games: piñata with naughty prizes—small cigarette packs, airplane liquor bottles, dollar bills; and spin the bottle still wearing the funny noses.

Full-Count B'day

Cynthia: Every year I take my grandmother, who lives in Florida, somewhere for her birthday. And every year I rack my brains to surprise her—which isn't easy because, at ninety-one, she's seen a lot. She's a major baseball fanatic and knows the batting averages of everyone on the Atlanta Braves. But her birthday's in February, before the season starts. So two years ago I took her and my family to spring training. Eight of us piled into a minivan and drove to Kissimmee, Florida. We tricked out the van with champagne, caviar and birthday cake, all in a cooler, and told her where we were going. She watched the training, mingled with the players, and the guy she's most crazy about came over and shook her hand. I don't think he'd ever seen a ninety-something baseball fan like my tiny grandmother.

Top This—Cakes

Lopsided, smudged, not enough room for the *y*. Are those supposed to be flowers? Never mind. Royal icing confections from the bakery may look grand, but they're also kind of bland. The funnier-looking the cake, the more you can taste the love. Which is why a Swell pastry chef excels at birthday cakes. She may not own a pastry bag or even a tip, but she has her own decorations, fixers and toppers to give the cake personality, help disguise screwups and, in case of emergency, make the store-bought look home-baked.

Toys and action figures: Tennis players, soldiers, a scuba diver—suit the toy to the birthday girl or boy. Create a tableau, like mini sailboats at a regatta, or a couple lounging under palm trees in hammocks and sprinkle green sugar crystals on the top layer to look like a lawn, or a hillock.

Sparklers: For an optical illusion, fill the whole cake with them and no ills are visible.

Edible Annuals: Find a bakery supply company in your town and pick up a garden variety of sugar flowers. Or you can make your own with candy supplies from the corner store—marshmallows and gumdrops. Slice the marshmallow crosswise, take each circular slice and pinch the ends to form petals, then place around a gumdrop or Dots center. Fresh pansies sold at gourmet produce sections are also pretty.

Cupcakes: Make a whole bunch, then give each a letter spelling out Happy Birthday, Diego!

Black and White: For your naughty-nice friend, lay a white angel food cake and

Gerbera Daisies. Plant those big, kindergarten-looking flowers right in the trouble spot or over the whole cake.

dark devil's food beside each other like a giant black-and-white cookie. Put an angel with a halo on one, a devil on the other.

Fast Food: If the b'day girl is a junk-food junkie, or you're in a pinch, build a cake using the old favorites: Yodels or Devil Dogs stacked like a pyramid, with candles.

Candyland Cake: In the absence of a facility for fondant swirls, make a plain cake dreamy by decorating the sides with jelly beans, spice drops, whips of licorice. . . .

Ice Cream Cake: Fudgy the Whale is hard to beat, but before Carvel had a wrap on ice cream cakes, they were popular homemade treats. And still really easy to make. Start with a spring form pan, then alternate layers of softened ice cream with strawberries, or crumbled chocolate wafers, or any sundae mix-in, then freeze and frost.

Sweet Birthday Suite

Cynthia: Hotels with restaurants are the perfect setting for surprise parties, as was proven at the surprise party I helped throw for Ilene's thirtieth birthday. Here was the ruse: an intimate formal dinner for eight in a small private room at 44, the restaurant at the Royalton Hotel in New York. She was thinking, *Wow! What a great party!* Unbeknownst to her, we'd also booked the penthouse party suite upstairs, and the other guests were filing in while we ate. We'd arranged with the hotel to serve hors d'oeuvres while we were downstairs in the curtained-off dining room. I'd say I had to go to the ladies' room and would check on everyone. After dinner, I pretended I knew the maitre d' and we

Hostess Cupcake

A few small touches can give the generic restaurant table more birthday flavor: funny birthday cards for place cards; a mound of gifts—favors for all the guests—cutely wrapped and heaped in the center of the table. Swap the birthday boy's china and glassware for a guest-of-honor setting—an oversized glass and a plate, giant napkin or a setting of bright striped dishware that stands out from the rest.

started talking about the hotel's new suites. He said, "Would you care to see one?" We said, "Love to!" He took us up and... Surprise! We'd decorated the room with blown-up photos of Ilene's first thirty years, supplied by her parents. My cousin Laura and I wrote a song called "We Love You, Ilene" (sung to the tune of Frankie Valli's "Can't Take My Eyes Off of You") and everyone joined in on   the chorus.

Two Restaurants Are Better Than One

Ilene: A restaurant-hop is another way to give a birthday dinner out some get-up-and-go. My sister, Debra, is obsessed with lobster, so to liven up the annual fancy dinner with the parents, we planned a Lobster Crawl. We kidnapped Debra at happy hour, with the B-52's "Rock Lobster" pumping on the car stereo. First stop was the new Red Lobster in Times Square, where we dived into lobster quesadillas, lobster pizza and giant Lobsterita drinks. At 7:50 sharp we scooted off to meet the parents at an upscale brasserie and loosened up the stuffy joint by pulling out our paper lobster bibs customized with the slogan DEBRA'S B'DAY. MAKE IT A 2-POUNDER! and telling the waiter to just bring on the lobsters and not slow us down with any fennel salad starters. We brought our own homemade chocolate cake decorated with a red-sprinkle lobster. For a gift, I gave Lobster Girl a pair of big red boxing gloves—so she could look the part. Debra hasn't eaten lobster since.

Throwing Your Own

Some people are reluctant to throw their own birthday party, as if it's asking for attention or something. But self-hostessing can be the way to have exactly the birthday you're in the mood for. The only downside is: no surprise. A mature way of having your b'day cake and eating it too is to organize your own but delegate one duty. Like the inviting.

Ask five favorite friends to invite five people each. Then you don't have to feel awkward asking everyone to come celebrate ME. And you can look forward to at least a few surprise guests.

Let's Go for a Ride

Ilene: The year *The Sopranos* debuted, I had my heart set on having my birthday at Manducatis, an Italian hangout in Queens where the mozzarella is always soft, the pinky rings flash and the prix fixe is affordable enough for a dozen friends *if* I pay in cash. I knew that trying to get my pallies to travel to some joint over the river would be a dealbreaker. Birthday or not, suddenly everyone would have a sick mother to feed, a cat to visit. So I planned a decoy and invited everyone to see the space show playing at the (then) brand-new Rose Center, and dinner afterward—leaving it vague where. After staring at the simulated galaxy for an hour and listening to Tom Hanks narrate the Big Bang, Queens didn't seem so far away, especially in a rented limo. Everyone piled in for cocktails under the moon roof and didn't ask questions.

Birthday Open House

Ilene: One year I'd been so busy that all I wanted for my birthday was a chance to see everybody. No big blast, just some time to hang out and make up for lost time. So I planned a Birthday Open House, inviting my friends and relatives to come visit any time between noon and midnight.

Feeding all those people for twelve hours actually didn't worry me. Having enough cool music did. DeeJaying all day seemed like so much effort. I wanted to keep the party vibe pumping even during a 2 P.M. social call. So I laid the responsibility on my guests. The invitation said "No gifts, please—but if you must, Ilene needs music! Bring a CD she should have in her collection." People loved getting such easy direction for what to bring. They downloaded special "Ilene mixes" or picked up CDs they loved, from Paris disco to obscure blues classics. When each guest arrived, I put his or her music on right away, which gave the party lots of mood shifts. And I learned surprising things about my friends' musical tastes. The best part was never being accountable. When it rocked, people were psyched to claim credit. When it sucked, I could pass the buck. "John's into didgeridoo—what can I tell you?"

Sentimentos

Birthdays that end with zero—the Big Ones—can be tricky. Helping the loved one get through the milestone can call for a dose of sentimentality mixed in with the revelry: something to tug at the heartstrings without opening a flood of candle-extinguishing waterworks.

A song or toast: People save them for weddings, but a birthday is a great opportunity for singing and roasting since there's far less pressure to be deep, meaningful or appropriate. Wake up a sedate dinner or create an intimate moment at a big affair with a song whose lyrics you reworked to suit the honoree. Pick a tune that's a funny fit and people will laugh at the first line: "If I Were a Rich Man" for your grandfather who, at eighty, still refuses to retire. And you can leave the guest-of-honor the lyrics as a souvenir.

Create a keepsake: Like an album. Ask friends to bring their favorite photo of themselves with the b'day boy or girl. Before the guest of honor arrives, have guests glue their pics into the book and sign the page—making a guest book and this-is-your-life album all in one. Fill remaining pages with snaps of the big night.

Funny face favors: Baby photos are sweet, but it could be more laughs if you incorporate the cute shots into souvenirs. Guests wear T-shirts with a different photo of Dad emblazoned on their chests. Or print that classic bearskin rug nudie shot on napkins for the b'day dinner. Serve the cake on commemorative plates that boast the b'day boy's hot high school yearbook pic, which guests only discover once they've finished their dessert.

Customize a game: Something to play after the cake's come and gone, like Two Truths and a Lie: Everyone writes down two facts and a falsehood about the b'day girl.

Cheesiest Birthday

Ilene: I'd made a lot of fancy dishes for my husband in my time but nothing to rival his obsessive—Oedipal?—attachment to his mother's macaroni and cheese. If he had to pick a last meal, no caviar, no Kobe beef, nor any other rarified delicacy could compete with those elbow noodles, cheddar sauce and ground beef in a casserole topped with golden homemade breadcrumbs. So when it came time to plan his birthday, I thought, give the boy what he wants! Not hauling Mom down from Toronto in her apron, but the next best thing—a Blue Ribbon bake-off. A blind taste test to find the best macaroni and cheese in New York.

Between restaurant guide books and word of mouth, we found the city's ten top mac 'n' cheese contenders and ordered a tray from each. We decanted them in silver chafing dishes lined up along the dining table and sideboard, and we gave each a number so guests would vote objectively on their favorite entrant. To give the bake-off a state fair feel, I cut cloth

No dish rivals my husband's obsessive— Oedipal?—attachment to his mother's macaroni and cheese.

napkins from gingham and tied on a rickrack apron, pinning the coveted blue ribbon to my hip. I'd never seen party guests more absorbed in a project. Forty people dutifully tasted, discussed and scored like judges at a state fair. And the mac 'n' cheeses were surprisingly distinct, from Artisanal, the city's high-end cheese specialists, to Michael Jordan's steak house to Anthony *(Kitchen Confidential)* Bourdain's Les Halles. Artisanal won the blue ribbon. The booby prize? Let's just say the only entry to fare worse than Cynthia's Kraft box special was my own attempt to replicate Rick's mom's. Though I still have my doubts that she gave me the real recipe.

Deck of Joy

Ilene: To ease the pain of hitting senior discount age, my mom, Joy, planned a weekend-long celebration at her house in Ocala, Florida. A dozen of her best friends flew in to fete her. All the friends of Joy contributed something—astrology readings, Reiki healing, channeling sessions. Since I have no official psychic talents or healing abilities, I came up with a game—a nostalgic version of Concentration.

My mom is obsessed with photos and has lived a very colorful life. So I did a Deck of Joy: fifty-two oversized playing cards with pictures from all the many chapters of her life. There were twenty-six different photos, so every card had a match. At the party, we dealt all fifty-two cards facedown on the floor. Players turned over two at a time, trying to make a match. If they turned over Joy in a swami robe from her ashram days, they had to remember where the other Swami Joy was. If they missed the match and got Joy in a beehive and maternity dress, the next player would be up. It was a great ride down memory lane, with lots of opportunities for Joy to tell stories and friends to ask about parts of her life they never imagined. Who's that foxy guy you're hugging in the sailboat? When did you marry a Japanese artist? You were *blond?*

The Not-So-Happy Birthday Song

What is it with "Happy Birthday to you"? How did that song, with its grating barbershop-quartet finish, "And many mooooore," become so popular? Written in 1893 by two schoolteacher sisters in Louisville, Kentucky, it's had a monopoly on the birthday business for more than a hundred years.

For those of us who always listen to the song with a groan, here are a few other options.

- "Today Is Your Birthday" (The Beatles), written in 5/4 time, which is why it's a much more upbeat b'day ditty
- "It's Your Birthday" (50 Cent)
- "Birthday" (Destiny's Child)
- "Birthday" (Blur)
- "It's My Birthday" (The Vandals, for the angst-inclined)

6 get-togethers

games night, book clubs,
viewing parties

play dates

These are parties in the loosest sense of the word. They're excuse-occasions to do something with your friends. Play games, watch TV, swap clothes—activity-based get-togethers to get away from the typical adult encounters in restaurants and bars, where everything is talk, eat, talk, drink, talk. Get-togethers are more like play dates—super low-maintenance because the "entertaining" is already taken care of, and ideal for school nights. With the focus on a pastime other than food and drink, those hostess responsibilities are secondary and minimal. Since the guests are your close pals, you could get away with walking into the living room with a bag of Tostitos in one hand, Oreos in the other. But it'll be worth it to give the casual affair and its surrounding snackery some panache, though not so much that you couldn't see turning it into a weekly ritual.

Let the Games Begin

Games Night – Party Armory

No matter how old people are, they still want to play at the house with the best toys. So clear a shelf or cabinet of any old computer bags, travel irons and other junk you were saving for no reason and make room for something more practical: games. Some old (Scrabble), some new (Cranium Turbo Edition) and, once you're on the lookout, novel vintage ones (Mystery Date, The "Laverne & Shirley" Game) uncovered at yard sales or in your parents' attic. The more you amass, the better shape you'll be in when you want to prolong an evening out but no one really feels like going to another club or bar. Games are a more chilled option, unless you're playing strip Operation.

To hold a more mixed group's interest and keep the party lively, set up a bunch of games. After one or two rounds, everyone jumps to the next one.

Bored Game Strategy: With even the best board games, sometimes after a few rounds a handful of players are no longer on board, so to speak. If your crowd shares a Monopoly obsession, by all means dig in for the night. But to hold a more mixed group's interest and keep the party lively, set up a bunch of games—Boggle, Pictionary, Trivial Pursuit. After one or two rounds, everyone jumps to the next game. Or go preverbal, let guests loose in a rec room of ages 8 to 12 games like Stratego, Battleship, Connect 4, Risk (the game of world domination!), Chinese checkers, Trouble! (everyone loves those poppin' dice),

Clue, Mastermind. Keep a Rubik's cube on the bar for the loner of the group.

Game Shows: Some of the best—and most competitive—games require no equipment at all. Celebrity and charades, unlike some of the more sedentary board games, can pump the room with game-show intensity.

If you have a crowd of eight or more, divide them into two teams. For celebrity, rip or snip a half dozen sheets of paper into small pieces. Each player gets about ten slips on which to write the names of famous people, living or dead. Fold the slips in half and throw them into a big bowl or hat. Now the first team goes. Set an egg timer or hourglass borrowed from another game for one minute. A member of the team pulls a piece of paper out of the hat and gives his teammates clues to guess the celeb's identity, trying desperately to get through as many names as pos-

sible in sixty seconds. For instance: "actor who always plays psychos . . . first name same as Jill's boyfriend in the nursery rhyme . . . made out with Diane Keaton"— until someone yells, "Jack Nicholson!"

The wide-ranging celebs can include not only Hollywood stars but also politicos, literary figures and historical figures, giving everyone a chance to shine, or not, like when you keep saying, "He's the secretary general of the UN!" to blank stares from your teammates. After all the names in the bowl are used up, tally the score. If you're really hardcore, add bonus rounds. Put all the names back in the bowl and start over—only this time, clues are limited to two words. For Madonna: "Material girl." The third round is no words, just mimed clues (and memory) and gets very silly.

The other game that gets people up and acting out is charades. Hollywood types play a variation called running charades, which is like a charades relay race, running from room to room. Another way to help branch out of the usual book titles and movies is to customize the game for your party with a theme: vacation destinations, fashion, great inventions.

Poker Night

In *The Odd Couple*, Felix drives Oscar and his poker buddies crazy when he prissifies their weekly slobfest by serving crust-free sandwiches, insisting on coasters and washing the cards. A Swell hostess does not Felix. Poker night is not a tea party. Even dips are dippy. But games do go on awhile, so you'll need sustenance. Something manly that necessitates no upkeep: *six-foot heroes.*

They'll be incredibly inexpensive and far more delicious if you make them at home. Buy a couple of the longest loaves of Italian bread you can find and deal out your favorite combos to cover the whole loaf: turkey, Jarlsberg, Russian, coleslaw, capicola, mortadella, provolone, red peppers, arugula, mozzarella. Move from meats on one end to vegetarian on the other. Stack the fillings as high as a Dagwood special and stab curly toothpicks to hold the loaf together before slicing. Pile chips on the side—the potato kind.

Now let's focus on the game: The hot one in poker circles is Texas hold 'em. That's what the pros play in the World Series of Poker, and it's the preferred game in those celeb tournaments Ben Affleck is always in. The basic rules are:

Each player is dealt two cards, facedown. A round of betting takes place: call, raise or fold. The dealer flips the next three cards faceup on the table. These are called the "flop," and are community cards. Eventually, five community cards will be placed faceup on the table. After the flop, there's another round of betting. The dealer plays one more faceup card on the table. This fourth community card is called the "turn" and begins the third round of betting. The dealer places the final faceup card on the table, called the "river." Players can now use any combination of seven cards—the five community cards and the two cards known only to them—to make the best possible five-card hand. After the final betting round, all players still in the game show their hands. The player who made the initial bet or the player who made the last raise shows her hand first. The player with the best hand wins a date with Ben Affleck.

Something to Offer

Since the fun and games generally take place on the later side of the evening, presumably everyone's already eaten, either at your house or before they came over, so there's no call for anything major. But a Swell hostess always has something to nibble and nip. To be ready to extend a spontaneous invite, deep-freeze ice cream, coffee cake, cookie dough and the number one favorite games night party food . . . bridge mix!

Later in the evening, when a whole new cocktail might seem too much, useful sipping drinks are Spanish sherry, brandies, Courvoisier, grappa—or any pretty mystery bottle you pick up on vacation. For these fetes, it also doesn't hurt to have a decent tea set, espresso machine or at least a set of coffee mugs that match.

Sweet Spot

As with cocktail fare, your all-you-can-sweet buffet will have more *oomph* if you think of one dessert concept and stick to it.

Easy-as-Pie Night: Spicy apple, peach, blueberry, lemon meringue, pumpkin, strawberry-rhubarb, banana cream. A row of pies warm from the oven or cool with fluffy tops will have a high wow factor. Boys in particular seem to get pie-eyed over

girls who make pie—it's that girl-next-door thing. The easiest recipe of course is finding a baker you believe in and just warming up the store-bought. For EZ Bake Level II: Buy ready-made frozen piecrusts—pastry, graham cracker, chocolate graham—and just make the fillings. To really fool 'em, grab your rolling pin and one of those excellent piecrust mixes in the box. Leave a flour-dusted rolling pin and apron on the kitchen counter just for effect. If you feel a need to go all the way, we've got a good crust recipe in the back of the book.

Puddings for Pudding: In England, they call dessert "pudding"—a good enough excuse to whip up a big pot of My-T-Fine and make some parfaits in your stemmed glasses, topped with whipped cream, a cherry, and ladyfingers.

Party Cake, Party Cake: Frosted cakes, like death-by-chocolate sugarfests, are so rich they knock you out with one slice for the rest of the night. Frosting-free coffee cakes are the ones guests come back for again and again. . . . The problem with them is that they're often in various shades of molasses, on the homely end of the baker's shelf. Whether baking or bakerying, steer toward cakes that look good enough to be put on a glass pedestal—lemon yellow pound cake dusted with confectioners' sugar or shimmery white coconut bundt cake topped with lots of shavings.

Sundae Night: A scooper and a tub of rock-hard ice cream isn't that exciting. Or easy on the guests. You'll get more enthusiasm from pre-scooped sundaes, like a triple shot of coffee ice cream served in those classic diner coffee cups with the IT IS OUR PLEASURE TO SERVE YOU slogan. You can pull them right out of the freezer. Serve alongside an array of toppings—whipped cream, hot chocolate sauce, chopped nuts, butterscotch sauce, crushed pineapple, chocolate covered espresso beans—from which guests can design their own sundaes.

Or grab the punch bowl and create one giant sundae with the works, the kind they used to serve at late-night date-night ice cream parlors, and had names like "The Kitchen Sink."

Pubwiches: In England and Ireland, pub crawlers while away hours playing darts and ranting poetically, fueled by a simple but steady diet of bite-size sandwiches on buttered white bread piled up in baskets, eaten by the dozen. They can fuel your party, too. Just a slice or two of filling with plenty of spice and sauce is a good alternative to the prosaic assorted wrap platters, which are as exciting as lunch hour. Pubwiches work best with dark, grainy breads that won't get soggy even when sliced very thin: for instance, baked ham chopped with English mustard and pineapple on rye, or rare roast beef with fresh horseradish cream on pumpernickel. Try chicken, chutney butter and chopped almonds on walnut raisin bread. Cheers.

Let's Get Lit

Now it can be told! The unspoken secret of book clubs is . . . no one reads the books. These "clubs" are yet another excuse-occasion for hanging out. But for the few minutes before the evening devolves into gossip and trash talk, find ways to keep even the delinquents involved. Out-loud readings add a performance element, and club members who didn't do their homework won't feel so guilty: At least they read those two pages. Make the reading material more spontaneous. Poems don't require advance reading time but can be digested on the spot, and they often provide neat segues to the topics really at hand—love, sex, depression. You can always dispense with the high-literary pretext and start with the gossip, reading only celebrity biographies. *Confessions of a Dangerous Mind*, the Chuck Barris memoir, or *Juiced,* Jose Conseco's pumped-up tell-all.

A harder question than what to read is what to serve: cheese or dessert? Dessert or cheese? Do both in one. At multistar restaurants, the desserts sound like the entrées and vice versa. With just a bit of extra effort, you can knock off an A+ cheese board. Whipped Brie sandwich cookies. Parmesan crisps, frico. Manchego and quince canapés. Apple-filled tartlets with cheddar topping. A little wheel of cheesecake with the book's name written on top.

Bitch and Swap

Clean out your closet and shop for a new look all in one evening. Everyone brings clothes to get rid of and throws them in a heap in the center of the room. Guests take a turn picking an item from the fashion heap. If no one else is interested, they're in luck: They can keep it. But if someone is, clear the catwalk! Pump up some hot runway music. Each guest models the item in question, doing their best Zoolander to work the look. The audience acts like fashion editors in a Roman Colosseum, giving the thumbs-up or thumbs-down. They decide with hoots, cheers, whistles, fashion tears and lots of gratuitous color commentary ("Girl, where you been hiding that bootay?"). Whoever looks best gets to keep the pink spectator pumps or macramé halter dress. Put out accessories—lipstick, heels, wigs, scarves, sunglasses—to help the competing "models" style up their looks. Serve lo-cal snacks: Zone bars and lots of (low-cal) white wine. For a favor, supply guests a new shopping bag, marked with their names, to take home their new wardrobe.

Clean out your closet and shop for a new look... all in one evening.

No Flipping

Season finales, award shows, big games . . . "Event TV" has entered our lives, and we do not like to watch alone. For these happy social occasions gathering around the electronic hearth, a Swell hostess is ready for her cameo.

TV, Dinner

Since most shows air during prime dinnertime, the goal is to civilize the dining experience so viewers aren't balancing napkins and plates of food in their laps. Get a few TV trays, the standing kind or cafeteria-style trays, and set them out on the buffet each fully set—napkin, silverware, glasses, flowers. Serve mood food and drinks that suit the show, and don't bother changing the menu from week to week. There's something very TV Land and comforting about eating the same thing every time you watch your favorite show.

The Sopranos: If ever there was a show that's all about the red sauce—"gravy," as the Jersey Italians say—this is it. Supermarkets now carry pretty good jarred stuff from classico Italian restaurants like Rao's and Patsy's, which can be doctored in less time than a commercial break to get a few steps closer to Mama's *cucina*. But if you've got time on Sunday afternoon to go from scratch, follow Clemenza's culinary advice to Michael in *The Godfather.*

> Heh, come over here, kid, learn something. You never know, you might
> have to cook for 20 guys someday. You see, you start out with a little
> bit of oil. Then you fry some garlic. Then you throw in some tomatoes,
> tomato paste, you fry it; ya make sure it doesn't stick. You get it to a
> boil; you shove in all your sausage and your meatballs; heh . . . ? And a
> little bit o' wine. An' a little bit o' sugar, and that's my trick.

Sex and the OC: The camera adds ten pounds. And so does watching whatever midriff-bearing, miniskirt-wearing fashion trend show happens to be in vogue this season. Open up a salad bar, California-style, meaning the less familiar the produce, the more fillingly slimming it'll taste. Everyone gets a big bowl to help themselves to: micro greens, fresh figs, avocado, sprouts, grapefruit, roasted sunflower or pumpkin seeds, slices of roast chicken, seared shrimp . . .

Chez Swanson. How much fun would it be to offer guests a long menu, from chicken tettrazini to fettucine Alfredo, and put everyone's dinner in the oven at once! But if in the reality show of your life your friends are too foodie for frozen TV dinners, make your own. Fill plates that have those dividers with your combination of down-home and take-home—fried chicken, mashed potatoes, green beans, a brownie. Or à la Boston Market, with Stovetop stuffing and cranberry sauce. Anyone got a recipe for Salisbury steak?

Superbowl: This is the one time of year most guys actually volunteer for kitchen duty, agonizing over their guacamole, bean dip and five-alarm salsas. Why interfere? Our suggested contribution to this potentially explosive buffet is little fingerbowls of antacids—your contribution to the Clean Air Act.

Oscar Night

The *chicks'* Super Bowl. Invite friends, family and other seat-fillers to dish the fashion, rate the up-dos, defend their favorite star's speech and gossip during commercials. Make yours the destination-viewing couch.

Stuff the (Invitation) Envelope, Please: Mylar mirrored paper addressed, "And the winner is . . ."; a note card inscribed in Oscar-gold metallic pen with a line from Oscar-winning films: "Maybe not now, maybe not tomorrow, but someday you'll regret . . . not showing up to our Oscar bash"; a red carpet swatch; card-stock punched with two holes through which you can loop some black ribbon into a black bow tie.

Dress the Set: Simulate Beverly Hills with palm plants on the champagne bar, covered in a few yards of silver lamé. Switch the family picks in the living room with shots of your true loved ones: Brad Pitt, Steve Martin, Gwyneth. The 8 x 10s are, of course, autographed (by you).

Mix Guests and Movie Trivia: At the bar, serve up trivia wine charms, cards with stumpers tied onto the flute stems. Guests must mingle to find the answers. Sample Q: Bette Davis won Best Actress for *All About Eve*, but which legendary sexpot also made her screen debut in the film? Marilyn Monroe. What movie did Bond creator Ian Fleming finally win an Oscar for? *Chitty Chitty Bang Bang!*

Food of the Gods: Bad enough we don't make $20 million a picture—do we have to be reminded of the fact by nibbling low-cal bean dip and Baked Lays while dreaming of stars feasting on nectar and ambrosia? Well, as it turns out, at the star-strewn Vanity Fair Oscar party, they serve LA's fave In-and-Out burgers. So why shouldn't you? To go with, make a Cobb salad, invented at The Brown Derby, a restaurant from Hollywood's golden era where having a phone call brought to your booth was the height of status, and Lucille Ball once had a food fight with dinner rolls. Owner Robert Cobb came up with the salad when a Hollywood big shot came in after the kitchen had closed and he had to raid the fridge for a midnight snack. To dress up the popcorn—mix up a punch bowl of Oscar ambrosia—butter-laced popcorn tossed with chocolates and dusted with edible gold leaf.

Goody Bags for the Worshipful: Include maps of stars' homes, celeb biographies—old and new—face powder, vintage sunglasses . . .

Splashing up the Oscar Pool: Once everyone's rushed to fill out their answers, nothing happens with the usual ballot drill. No one wins until the marathon broadcast is over and everyone can't wait to go home. But what if before the show, you give each guest a bag filled with poker chips. Guests place their bets when the nominees are announced. If one person wins, he or she gets all the chips. A tie shares the pot, and so on. There's a winner every round, and whoever has the most chips at the end of the show wins the grand prize: Blockbuster gift certificate . . . a free Botox treatment.

The Invitation: Mylar mirrored paper addressed, "And the winner is . . ."

And the winner is

Celebrity Deathmatch Premiere Party

Ilene: Blood, guts, gore—time to celebrate! My then-boyfriend Rick and his writing partner, A.J., had just gotten their big break. A show they'd written was going to air on national television! Okay, it was an episode of MTV's *Celebrity Deathmatch*, in which a claymation Oliver Stone and Martin Scorsese climbed into a wrestling ring to battle to the death. But a girlfriend has to be supportive. I threw them a premiere party!

The VIP list was our friends and relatives. We rented a red carpet from a prop house and ran it down the hallway to our apartment door. To get everyone in the mood for the show I did a violence-themed menu with lots of bad puns and title cards so no one would miss the jokes: Bloody Marys and "Knock-out" Punch; Arti-Choke Dip, Black-Eyed Peas, Cauliflower-Ear Pie, Kung Pow Chicken (sweet-spicy Kung Pao ordered from a Chinese restaurant and skewered into hors d'oeuvres). For dessert, we had loaves of pound cake and a big bowl of jawbreakers.

7

blowouts
new years
to
bachelorettes

the big bang theory

For certain holidays and life events, a big bang is the only way to go. On those occasions, volume counts: music, voices, hair and the sheer thrill of the throng. Strangers socialize more when they're thrust together with maximum PPSF (people per square foot) and minimum lighting. Low lights and great sound are emboldening. The Swell impresario manages the Big Party so that it's not a mob you want to escape but an intoxicating scene where guests drag each other to the dance floor shouting, "What's your name?"

Venue

Having a Big Party in a Small Space

You don't need a 3,000-square-foot apartment with an acre of balcony. In some ways the humble abode is even better suited to a big blast, because you can achieve the madding crowd vibe and look incredibly popular with far fewer guests. To magnify the petite party palace . . .

Deconstruct the bar. Rather than have one big bar, serve self-contained bevies—champagne splits, bottled beer, soda—in improvised ice buckets set up all around the apartment.

Clear the decks. In party spaces where real estate is at a premium, get rid of all stuff you are not going to use. Stow photos and bric-a-brac to make as much surface space as possible for candles, flowers, drinks. Put the TV in the closet and use the trolley for serving snacks. Push furniture to the sides of the room, ballroom style, leaving an open area for standing and dancing.

Take back the bedroom. Instead of turning it into a horizontal closet, rent a coat rack for the hallway and reclaim that wasted real estate. It makes a cute hangout zone if you can cover the bed with something less delicate and private looking than your actual sheets and duvet: a fur throw, afghans and cushions imported from the living room. Add an incentive: Put some candles on the end table with glasses and something fun to drink, some French brandy, a bottle of champagne cooling. Open up a backgammon board, or other game, a Polaroid camera and an empty photo album/guest book.

Sound Check

Make sure you have enough music for the whole night. Figure three minutes a song. When self-deejaying, approach the music as you would the food and drink, giving the tunes a point of view. No need to get into the Wedding Band mentality of a little bit to please everyone—Motown on down. It'll be easier to find a playlist on your iPod or own CD collection if you pick a concept and stick to it—at least for a little while. Plan a few thematic shifts through the night so there's a beginning, a middle and an end, the end probably being the

A big party pretty much lives and dies by the music. Organize your tunes in advance.

rowdiest. The theme could be a period—eighties dance music. Disco. Emo. Or it could just be a mix of artists and bands you love right now. A playlist riff could be inspired by lyrics—only songs that include a particular word, say, *Love*. When your dance tunes are starting to roll in, turn the lights down and the volume up.

Going Live

There's nothing like live musicians to shoot energy into a party. But don't wait to be having one to start talent scouting. If you're at a bar with a cool deejay, a club with a fun band, or on the subway platform tossing coins to some amazing trumpet player—tell them you love their music and get their number. Having the music may even be inspiration to have a party. It doesn't have to be too loud or expensive if you just hire one or two musicians. If you don't stumble across anyone, scour the back of the local city magazine for a two-piece steel band, a bongo player, a Theramin prodigy, a Bulgarian deejay.

Get Help!

Few things are sadder than the sight of one of those self-serve bar tables mid-bash with capsized two-liter soda empties and guests mixing vodka drinks with no mixers or ice. If you recognize any of these signs, you need to seek professional help.

The bar must remain neat and inviting all night long. It is your hold on civilization.

Booze calculator

How much you'll need:
- *Guestimate two drinks a person per hour.*
- *One bottle of wine pours about six glasses.*
- *A quart of booze makes about sixteen drinks.*
- *Nothing says party's over like running out of ice and glasses. Don't skimp—one pound of ice per person per hour, and one glass per person per hour. Generally, you'll go through less ice if you chill the mixers.*
- *If you're still unsure, make nice to the liquor store clerk: he or she should know how much wine and spirits you'll need for the amount of guests and length of your party. While you're at it, have ice and booze delivered. You'll buy more if you're not looking at it and don't have to carry it.*

An Ice Man Cometh: If you're expecting thirty people or more, pony up for a bartender. Rope in some cohosts to defray the cost if necessary. You won't regret it. Once you've hired someone, all you need to supply is a small cutting board, a sharp knife, a large ice scoop and you're free. A Swell hostess makes a point of knowing the names of the staff members so that she can be polite when addressing them or offering their services: "Let Gino fix you a drink . . ."

Deus Ex Machina: You can also upgrade the usual self-serve situation with a bar that's high-concept and low-maintenance. A pair of frozen margarita machines, then you don't need a bartender. Proper curvy margarita glasses, pre-salted, and fruit garnishes will add a touch of class. For an after-hours fantasy, rent a trio of water coolers filled with punch, appletinis or cosmos. Guests just turn the tap and the cocktail pours out nice and chilled, giving people even more reason to hang out by the watercooler. Ice sculpture bars—ironic, maybe, but it's definitely a memorable splurge to have an iced champagne fountain at the New Year's party, or citron vodka spraying from Cupid's love wand at the engagement bash. You can explore party-rental websites and classifieds for munchie machines you might normally only look at if you were having a second bat mitzvah: a frozen ice-cream machine, a cotton-candy machine, popcorn machine, donut machine. . .

Glass Is Class: Though the temptation when thinking of a big party is to get away with plastic, the style upgrade that comes with serving cocktails in glasses is like going from a Louis Vuitton knockoff to the real thing. Rent them. It's worth the expense if you can swing it. There's nothing dreamier for a hostess than having the rental company come and pick up all the unwashed the morning after. The all-purpose glass to get is a ten-ounce stemmed glass. But the beauty of a rental company is to indulge your whims. If your party hat is set on one special cocktail—maybe your signature cognac elixir—rent only the balloon glasses.

Explore party-rental websites for munchie machines you might normally only look at if you were having a second bat mitzvah.

Blastoffs

The Boo-tiful People

Halloween parties for adults can be scary. Six people turn up in costumes. All that *Children of the Corn* décor. We'd rather make the setting frighteningly chic, taking inspiration from Truman Capote's legendary black-and-white masked ball, five hundred of New York and Hollywood's highest society partying all night at the Plaza hotel. Invite everyone to come to your place in their most glamorous black-and-white. For a Halloween twist, make it a black-*light* party, so that everything white has an eerie glow. Leave it to the guests to decide if they prefer beautiful gowns and great masks or actual black-and-white costumes. The pregnant nuns, bloody nurses, mummies and Playboy bunnies will all appear cooler. Cover the furniture with white drop cloths. They look great, and are excellent for cleanup. Add décor to the dark with full white roses and spray-on spiderwebs. Trick the place out with black-and-white treats: a block of white marshmallow with dark chocolate fondue, black-and-white cookies. *Mmm*, spooky.

Decadent New Year's

The key to a Happy New Year's is to take the pressure off. It doesn't have to be the Best Party of the Year. It just has to be a little more louche, wanton, decadent than the usual. After all, it's the last night on the calendar, and tomorrow starts with all those good intentions to be a better person, to hit the treadmill, to call your mother. Make it a night worthy of repenting.

Invitation: Send out a little mirror or round piece of shiny Mylar paper on which you write Time to Reflect.

Break Resolutions: At the start of the party, each guest makes a resolution for the following year and writes his or her vice on a name tag— Smoking, Chocoholism, Swearing, Kissing Boys I Don't Know. Then spend the rest of the evening breaking it—with support from your fellow partiers—till midnight, that is.

Look Filthy Rich: Wear the most luxurious thing you own, even if it's not completely in style—a fur coat with only a slip underneath, all your "family heirloom" jewelry—tiara, bangles and other big baubles. (So what if they're all fakes?) The boys can do ascots, Brylcreemed hair, pinky rings, boutonnieres and lots of cologne.

Charm Good Fortune: Every culture has a good-luck ritual for the new year. Adopt the most decadent ones: the Spanish wear yellow

It doesn't have to be the Best Party of the Year. It just has to be a little more louche, wanton, decadent than the usual.

underwear, and Italians throw a bucket of water out the window—not to mention busted alarm clocks and any other out-with-the-old junk.

Look for a Silver Lining: Fill the ceiling with Mylar balloons. Cover the table with leftover Christmas tree tinsel.

Caviar Dream Puffs: Come up with one dreamy treat and go to town—something elegant that you love. It could be roast squab, oysters Rockefeller, a chocolate bomb. For our money it's cream puffs—caviar cream puffs, chocolate cream puffs . . . puffs all party long.

Extreme Playlist: Spin the most popular songs of the year—and the biggest bombs. This gives everyone a chance to groan and groove and catch up on the ones they missed. Encourage mingling by interspersing your playlist with songs with the word new in them—even if they're tonal non sequiturs. Every time one of the "new" lyrics comes up—"What's new, pussycat?"—guests on the dance floor have to change partners. When "New Years Day" by U2 comes up, change again.

G'bye Party

When somebody's leaving town, what better gift than to help 'em pack up? Or at least create the illusion, sort of like your parents did when you said you were running away from home. Find vintage valises in all shapes and sizes from the flea market and fill them with party supplies. Make one the bar filled with bottles on one side, glasses on the other. Another suitcase serves as bread basket. A round vanity case can display the so-long cake. Finally, have a suit-

Bubbly Bar

De-Flatten the usual bubbly by making a champagne bar the centerpiece of the party with fixings for classic champagne cocktails and your new creations.

- *Bellinis: Peach puree and a bit of bubbly.*
- *Black velvet: Champagne flute half-filled with dark Guinness draft and finished with champagne. Good for a good-bye party, because it was invented about 150 years ago in London when England was in mourning for Prince Albert by a bartender who felt the champagne ought to be in mourning, too.*
- *Mimosa: Fresh orange juice filling a quarter of a frosted flute, add 2 dashes of Grand Marnier and finish with champagne. Named after the Mimosa tree because the cocktail should have the same color as its yellow blossoms. Wake it up with pineapple juice.*
- *Kir Royale: Crème de cassis and champagne. Bright pink cocktail with bubbly head, our Pink Lady.*
- *Lainesborough: Passion fruit juice and cranberry in equal parts. A splash of Grand Marnier. Top with champagne. Shake.*
- *Death in the Afternoon: 5 oz. champagne and a half ounce of Hemingway's poison, Pernod. Garnish with a twist.*

case plastered with tourist stickers from your hometown, or city, and pack it up with sentimental mementos. Have the guests bring something to remember the guest of honor by, a concert ticket stub, the lighter they always borrowed, a piece of the plastic fruit they always made fun of. And a g'bye album. Designate a paparazzo to snap a Polaroid of each guest waving, then have them write their adios message beside it. Throw in a packet of Kleenex before snapping the case closed and bidding bon voyage.

Cupid Party

There are so many people you wanted to fix up over the year but never got around to. Well, Valentine's Day isn't the only occasion for spreading the love. Invite all your unmatched friends, and let them know there's someone at the party you want them to meet, but don't say who. At the beginning of the party each guest gets a matchbook with two clues about his or her match. Guests spend the party trying to find their fix-up and on the way meet lots of people. To loosen people up, hire artist's models to pose as cupids, seminude with bows and arrows, and have lots of sketchbooks and charcoals handy. Give aphrodisiacal cocktails—Love Potions Number 9, 10 and 11—and lubricate the love-song soundtrack. Guests find out their fix-up on the way out with a favor envelope holding the name and polaroid of their potential paramour.

Splash!

Truth is, at a nighttime party around the pool people rarely swim. Who wants to wreck their hair and makeup? Well, if no one's swimming, might as well put the pool to good use.

• *Aqua Centerpiece:* Make it a giant vase filled with flowers and floating candles for a romantic starry night. Hire synchronized swimmers for entertainment, or just get beach balls and blow-up toys if your vibe's more pop.

• *I Scream for . . .* Set coolers and ice buckets all around the grounds filled with Good Humor ice cream bars, nutty buddies, strawberry shortcakes, frozen candy bars, Mario's ices, Dove bars, chipwiches.

• *Freestyle Punch:* Fill the punchbowl with all the fruits in season, premarinated for extra punch, and scoops of fruity sorbets drifting on top.

• *The Drinks Are Cold, but the Hostess Is Hot:* Seize the opportunity to look casual but super glam in a long hostess skirt, bikini top and dangly earrings. Wear mules or flat sandals, better for the grass.

Get a Room!

One obvious but overlooked way to throw a carefree bash is to have it somewhere other than your house. Like in a hotel room. Hotels are sexy. Mysterious. Anonymous. For the same amount it would cost to buy booze and hire a bartender chez toi, you could rent a suite: a room with a view, room service! We tried this idea out for our first book party celebrating the publication of *Swell: A Girl's Guide to the Good Life*. And, best of all, when the party's over, you can just put a few bucks on the dresser and walk out the door. Let housekeeping deal with the morning-after mess.

Setup

The only trouble is the bed, which can hog a lot of valuable party space in a hotel room. The only way is to use it. We had a few rooms at one of the W hotels in midtown Manhattan while the hotel was still under construction, and tricked out each room with a theme inspired by one of the chapters of the book.

The Love Room: We loaded the bed with boxes and more tiny golden boxes of Godiva chocolates, a big diary started with a couple of steamy entries and a pen. Guests lounged about popping bonbons and adding lusty bits to the diary saga. It turned out like an R-rated guest book.

The Have-Fun Room: A pillow fight room, overflowing with so many white pillows that you could barely make out where the bed was. We scribbled quotes from the book on the pillowcases with laundry marker, mixed with cute pillow talk: "Was it good for you?"

Nibbles—Room Service!

Rather than order up a boring cheese plate or have the kitchen make up pricey and excessively fancy hors d'oeuvres, we ordered items from the regular room service menu—in party-friendly portions. Easy if you're willing to sound like you have a major eating disorder. "Could we have five grilled cheese sandwiches cut into thirty pieces, please, and toothpicks in each one? Thanks!" The waiters walked around with the grilled-cheese squares, whole trays of French fries, teacups of tomato soup.

Action/Playing It Safe

Forgoing favors or goodie bags, we got a prize for each room instead and hid it in the safe. We wrote up Swell trivia quizzes (good excuse for guests to talk), the answers to which provided the combination. How many times did Zsa Zsa Gabor marry? At the blackjack table a good player "splits" her hand if she draws a pair of what card? And so forth. The guest who solved the quiz first would crack the safe and win the loot inside.

Small-Scale Blowouts

Blackout Party

Cynthia: I was at work in Midtown when the blackout of 2003 happened. There were sixteen people in my office with nowhere to go, so I suggested that we walk to my apartment. Before we left, I wrote my address on everyone's hand in case we got separated. We walked fifty-something blocks downtown, but when we got to my place, I realized that I didn't have anything to serve them. I tried to cook everything in the refrigerator that was about to go. I took all this cheese—even the Kraft singles my daughter eats—and put it in a fondue pot with a little milk and heated it with a candle. It worked! Then I went to the deli. It was closed, but I talked them into letting me buy some salads and chips. We had red wine, which you can drink at room temperature, and we put candles everywhere—some stuck in beer cans, some in brown paper bags, some on plates. Later, I put out pillows and beddings for everyone (I have wall-to-wall carpeting, so it's kind of cushy), and we told ghost stories because we were in the dark, obviously, and it was a little scary. Talk about embracing imperfection.

Bachelorette Parties

Does the bachelorette party need to be as tawdry as the traditional bachelor bacchanal, or is there a better way for women to take advantage of the final hours of freedom? This is probably the last time you can just disappear without explaining yourself. So, plan a Runaway Weekend on Travelocity: Paris and everybody chips in on a hottie outfit for the bride-to-be's last night out. Or a road trip to rediscover her high school haunts. Or to the pistol range. What a great time to

The Blackout of 2003—
16 people in my office
with nowhere to go…
I suggested that we
walk to my apartment.

learn to use a gun! Make targets of the bride's old boyfriends and pretend you're Charlie's Angels on a mission to expunge her past once and for all.

Ilene: When my number came up and it was time to walk the plank, take the plunge, put on the old ball and chain, Cynthia and my sister, Debra, organized a going-away party. My only request was *not* the traditional bachelorette revel that inevitably ends sloshed in a bar, asking guys to nibble my candy necklace. So they organized a more romantic affair.

The girlfriends and I were all spirited off to a mystery destination—the wild blue yonder, by balloon. I was having a perfectly nice time sipping champagne over rural New Jersey when suddenly Cynthia's cell phone rang. Just as I was giving her a look for taking calls during my bucolic sail, she said, "It's for you." I recognized the voice instantly. Benny—my college sweetheart. We hadn't spoken in at least ten years! Cynthia had tracked him down, got past his wife and convinced him to ring at the appointed time. I cried right away as we reminisced, and he offered a few wise words about marriage—all the more startling since I didn't know he was already a dad with two kids. We were just making lunch plans when, as fate would have it, we lost the connection. What a swell way to celebrate the end of my single life, saying good-bye to my first great love. I was blown away. Then the phone rang again. "Mitchell?"

Party Proofing

To avoid getting your place trashed:

- *Place a doormat outside the front door.*
- *When moving furniture, lift, don't slide.*
- *Have a couple of trash cans in the kitchen. Most accidents happen when drinks are stacked up on top of the stereo, etc.*
- *Watch what you serve. If the crowd is big, expect droppage and squishage under heels. So don't serve things that stain. Nothing red—no berries, no red drinks, whether wine or cocktail.*

When all that fails, and you serve cranberry sangria cocktails:

- *Rub scuff marks with a nylon pad, dishwashing liquid and water or a pencil eraser.*
- *Harden candle wax with ice, then pry off with a flat knife.*
- *Soak beverage stains in cool water. Spritz with your prewash stain remover before running through the washing machine.*
- *Place a paper towel on lipstick smudges and sponge with dry-cleaning solvent.*
- *Place a white paper towel on pen marks and sponge with dry-cleaning solvent or rub some detergent into the area.*
- *Don't mix. Ammonia and chlorine bleach, for instance, can blow up, which could be hazardous to your next blowout.*

Before You Go

And now...the end is near...so don't forget to re-cy-cle. Hope you leave this party book with a favor bag filled with ideas for a few of your own brunches and blowouts. But even if you never have anybody over, Swell party logic can be applied to dressing up the days in between parties, like smuggling a bottle of vino and glasses in your attaché onto the commuter train to start

the weekend early, using hostess introductions or flirty conversation starters at someone else's affair. But do us a favor. Have a party. And send us a Polaroid!

Recipes

Banana Bread by the Yard

- 3 1/2 cups flour
- 4 teaspoons baking powder
- 1/2 teaspoon baking soda
- 1 teaspoon salt
- 1 1/3 cups sugar
- 2/3 cup shortening
- 4 eggs, well beaten
- 1/2 teaspoon vanilla extract
- 6 bananas, mashed
- 1/2 cup chopped nuts

First order of business: Get two 16-inch-long bread pans. Preheat oven to 350 degrees F. Sift flour, baking powder, baking soda and salt. Mix sugar and shortening until light and fluffy. Add eggs and vanilla and beat well. Mix in dry ingredients and bananas until smooth. Add nuts. Turn into greased pans. When both loaves are done, splice them together into a yard of bread (well, 32 inches, but who's counting?).

Jammin' Muffins

Give muffins from the mix a homemade spin with your own jam filling. Fill muffin trays halfway with corn batter, add a dollop of jam, then fill rest of tin with batter. Bake a couple minutes more than usual. When you bite into one, it's like a jelly donut.

Strawberry Jam-boree

Homemade strawberry jam is supercinchy to make if you're not preserving it with wax seals in airtight jars to store in the root cellar for the long winter. Make just enough for brunch in seconds.

- 2 pints strawberries
- 1 cup sugar
- 1/4 cup water

Combine all ingredients in a saucepan and cook over low heat until really dense and jammy. The end.

Tutti-Fruity Lemonade

- 5 cups water
- 1/2 cup sugar
- 2 cups fresh lemon juice
- 2 cups strawberries, cherries or blueberries

Heat 1 cup water and dissolve sugar; pour into pitcher. Add rest of water, lemon juice and fruit. Since lemonade can never be cold enough, freeze the fruit and plop in as additional ice cubes. Or . . .

Splash Up Store-Bought

- 6 scoops Country Time, or other lemonade mix
- 2 quarts water
- 1 pint strawberries
- Dash of cayenne—the magic ingredient that cuts the store-bought taste and makes everyone thirsty for more.

Fill blender with all ingredients and blend.

Hail Bloody Mary

- 1 quart tomato juice (or half tomato, half V8)
- 1/2 cup fresh lemon juice (two lemons, squeezed)
- 2 tablespoons horseradish
- Ground pepper
- Several shakes of Worcestershire sauce and Tabasco
- 1 1/2 cups vodka

Mix all ingredients together. To serve, rim glasses with lemon juice and celery salt. Garnish with celery stalk, Kirby cuke, olives, something green. Swap vodka for tequila and call it a Bloody Maria. With Clamato it's a Bloody Caesar.

Breakfast Pizza

(Serves 4)

- 8 slices bacon
- 16 mushrooms, cleaned, sliced
- Fresh pepper
- 8 eggs
- 2 tablespoons ketchup
- Several shakes Tabasco
- 4 8-inch Boboli or other pizza crust
- 1 1/2 cups grated cheddar cheese

Preheat oven to 400 degrees F. Fry bacon until crispy; remove from pan. Drain excess fat, leaving some drippings to sauté mushrooms. Pep up 'shrooms with fresh pepper and remove from pan. Scramble eggs. Mix ketchup and Tabasco sauce to taste and spread thinly on pizza crusts. Distribute eggs, sprinkle cheddar and layer on mushrooms and crumbled bacon. Bake 8 to 10 minutes. Looks like a delicious pizza, tastes like breakfast.

When Irish Coffee's Smiling

Pour 1 jigger Irish whiskey into a coffee cup. Add 2 teaspoons sugar and strong black coffee. Top with sweetened whipped cream. For a softer wake-up call, sub creamy Bailey's Irish Cream for whiskey.

Western Omm-let

In Italy it's a frittata, in Spain a tortilla—either way the round, thick omelet that can be served warm or room temperature, sliced like a pie for brunch or appetizer, gives a hostess peace of mind because you can dress it up with any combination of delicacies or use up leftover scraps from the refrigerator. Here's one of each kind, fancy and foraged:

Green Leeks and Ham

- 10 eggs
- 3 leeks
- 2 tablespoons extra virgin olive oil
- 1 potato, sliced
- Salt
- 1 thick slice ham
- Herbs

Whisk eggs until frothy. Slice leeks—the whites and a bit of green—into rings and sauté in oil until very soft and sweet. Add potato slices, sprinkle with salt and cook until tender. Add hammy bits and any herbs on hand to egg mixture, pour into the pan and stir. Now flip the frittata! Loosen the bottom and slide it onto a large plate; cover with another plate and turn upside down. Remove top plate and slide the half-cooked frittata back into pan, raw side down, and cook over medium heat for another few minutes, until the bottom looks brown when you take a peek. Slide onto a serving dish.

Queen Crab

- 10 eggs
- 1 teaspoon salt
- Pepper
- 1 tablespoon olive oil
- 3 tablespoons minced shallots
- 1 1/2 cups tomatoes, diced (2 tomatoes)
- 1/3 cup sliced basil
- 2 teaspoons fresh thyme
- 1/2 pound fresh crabmeat

Whisk eggs until frothy and season with half the salt and pepper.

In a 10-inch skillet, heat olive oil to medium heat and sauté shallots for a minute or two until just starting to turn golden. Add tomatoes and herbs, raise heat and cook until the tomato water is evaporated. Stir in crabmeat; season with remaining salt and pepper.

Add eggs, stirring with wooden spoon, and cook over lowish heat until they're set but still soft on top. Let set, flip, slide back into pan, brown.

Cooking Tip: If you can't master the flipping, another way to go is to slip the skillet into the oven and brown the top under the broiler (make sure the handle is flameproof).

Pot o' Chai

- 2 tablespoons grated fresh ginger

- 1 stick cinnamon

- 8 cloves

- 8 peppercorns

- 4 cups cold water

- 6 bags black tea

- 1 cup milk

- 2 tablespoons honey, or sugar

Soak spices in water for 1/2 hour, boil, add tea. Let steep 10 minutes, strain, add milk, bring to boil, add honey or sugar to taste. Bring to boil again. Great served iced with whipped cream, too.

Thelma and Louise Wafflewiches

(Serves 6)

- 12 Eggo waffles

- 8 eggs

- 12 slices bacon

- Maple syrup

Toast waffles (instead of bread). Scramble eggs, fry bacon. Spoon eggs in center of waffles. Lay two slices bacon, drizzle with warmed maple syrup, cover with second waffle and wrap each individually in aluminum foil to keep the heat in.

Shrimp from the Old Bay

- Olive oil

- Lemon juice

- 1 pound jumbo shrimp

- 1 tablespoon Old Bay seasoning

Mix olive oil and lemon in a big Tupperware or bowl, throw in shrimp and Old Bay seasoning. You don't even have to shell them. Coat shrimp well. Heat a big nonstick skillet on medium high, and toss in shrimp. Flip after 2 minutes or until the shells get all orangey pink. When cool enough to handle, skewer shrimp with wooden skewers and wrap in Saran Wrap and aluminum foil. Refrigerate until P-time.

"Hot" Deviled Eggs

(See page 192)

Bill-ionaire's Bacon Jerky

(Makes about 36 pieces)

- 1/2 pound thick-cut bacon

- 2 tablespoons dark brown sugar

Heat oven to 375 degrees F. Line two baking sheets with aluminum foil. Cut each slice of bacon into thirds. Toss bacon with sugar; place on baking sheet and bake about 6 to 8 minutes, turning once, until crispy and brown. Serve with cocktails.

Salmon Spread and Celery "Chips"

(Makes 1 1/2 cups)

- 1 package (8 ounces) cream cheese, softened
- A few slices smoked salmon
- 1 tablespoon fresh lemon juice
- 6 ribs celery, sliced in 1/4 inch diagonal "chips"

Combine cream cheese, salmon and lemon juice in food processor until smooth and pink. Serve in a bowl surrounded by celery. Use inner sprigs of celery leaves for garnish.

Mealwiches

The Swell way to avoid knives and forks is to serve a whole picnic between two slices of bread.

Crispy Chicken and Appleslaw

(Makes 10)

Appleslaw:

- 1 lb coleslaw
- 1 tablespoon cider vinegar
- 2 apples in season, cored, sliced
- 1/2 cup toasted walnuts

Combine ingredients in a large bowl and toss well; season with salt and pepper. Cover and refrigerate.

Chicken Slices:

Use fried chicken breasts (from your favorite takeout. If no such place exists, follow directions below).

- 1 cup bread crumbs

- 1 tablespoon chili powder

- 1 teaspoon salt

- 1 teaspoon pepper

- 1/2 cup all-purpose flour

- 2 eggs, lightly beaten

- 10 boneless chicken cutlets (4 ounces each)

- 1/2 cup olive oil

Combine bread crumbs, chili powder, salt and pepper on a dish or wax paper. Lay out another sheet of wax paper for flour. Beat two eggs with a splash of water. Dredge chicken in flour, dip in eggs, then coat with bread-crumb mixture. Use a fork to handle the chicken so the batter doesn't gum up on your hands.

In a large skillet heat half the oil. Fry the chicken in batches, 5 to 6 minutes each, depending on the size of the breasts, turning once. Add additional oil if needed. Smear honey mustard on insides of rolls and stack with chicken and appleslaw.

Steak au Poivre and "Salad"

(Serves 10)

- 1 cup mayonnaise

- 1/4 cup white horseradish, drained

- 1 1/2–2 pounds sirloin steak, trimmed

- 1 tablespoon olive oil

- 2 tablespoons coarse black pepper

- 1 teaspoon salt

- 2 sourdough baguettes

- 1 bunch watercress, cleaned and trimmed

Prepare grill or heat broiler. In small bowl mix mayonnaise and horseradish; set aside. Rub steak with oil, then pepper and salt. Grill 6 to 8 minutes for medium-rare, turning once. Let stand 10 minutes; cut across the grain in thin slices. Pull dough from baguettes. Spread hollowed baguettes with horseradish mixture; top with steak and watercress. Slice into manageable-size sandwiches and fasten with a curly toothpick.

Pink G&T

Rub lime wedge around rim of a highball glass, fill with ice, pour 1 1/2 ounces gin and top off with tonic. Add a splash of grenadine to turn it pink. For full preppy effect do a green "fruit salad" garnish with limes or kiwi or some such on skewers. Do not stir. It ruins the carbonation and the buzz. Alcohol in a bubbly drink will hit you faster than in its still version.

Cocoa Chanel

(Serves 6)

The Aztecs invented hot chocolate, and drank it fiery with chili peppers. Cortés brought it back to Europe, where they added sugar and spices like cinnamon, black pepper, orange flower water, powdered roses and almonds. Zing up the Swiss Miss and Nestlé's with a few cinnamon sticks or vanilla bean. Or, for a really rich, old-fashioned Parisian tea salon quality hot chocolate . . .

- 2 cups milk
- 1/2 cup heavy cream
- 1/4 cup unsweetened cocoa powder
- 6 ounces semisweet chocolate
- 1 teaspoon vanilla
- whipped cream, or marshmallows

In a saucepan warm the milk, cream and cocoa. Over medium heat, add chopped chocolate and stir until it melts. Lower heat to a simmer and cook another 5 minutes. Remove from heat, add vanilla and serve with whipped cream or marshmallows.

Football Snaps

- 3/4 cup butter
- 1 cup brown sugar
- 1/4 cup molasses
- 1 egg
- 2 1/4 cups flour
- 2 teaspoons baking soda
- 1/2 teaspoon salt
- 1 teaspoon ginger
- 1 teaspoon cinnamon
- 1/2 teaspoon cloves

Preheat oven to 375 degrees F. Cream butter, sugar, molasses and egg until fluffy. Sift dry ingredients. Stir in molasses mixture until blended. Form small balls and pinch the ends. Bake for 10 minutes. Let cool, then decorate with white icing X's (the laces) along one side.

Kabobs-Your-Uncle

Beef, pork or chicken cut into 1 1/2-inch cubes (Make pork pieces a little smaller, because they have to cook more thoroughly.)

Marinade Sauce

- 1 cup light soy sauce
- 1/2 cup cider vinegar
- Pineapple juice
- Light brown sugar
- 2 teaspoons salt
- 1 teaspoon garlic, pureed (The tube variety works fine and is easier to handle than actual cloves. A hint of garlic goes a long way on social occasions.)

Marinate meat and chicken for a couple of hours in the refrigerator.

Fill skewers with fruit and vegetables—cherry tomatoes, shallots, pineapple, mushrooms, squash—which go between meats, not only because they're tasty, but because they allow hot air to circulate so the meat cooks well.

Fruit Kabobs

- Fresh fruit (plums, peaches, figs, strawberries, rhubarb—whatever's most in season), cut into bite-size chunks

Arrange fruit on platter. Guests can thread their own skewers. Arrange kabobs on edges of grill over indirect flame. Brush fruit with basting sauce (1 cup melted butter, 3/4 cup apricot preserves and a squeeze of lemon). Arrange on grill, cover and cook 3 to 5 minutes, or until lightly brown. Sprinkle with coconut.

Wine-and-Cheese Burgers

- 2 pounds lean chuck or sirloin, ground
- 2 teaspoons salt
- 1/4 teaspoon black pepper
- 1/4 cup red wine
- 1/4 cup tomato juice
- 3 ounces Roquefort cheese, crumbled, or a cubed Gouda

Mix cheese and other ingerdients into meat, shape into 6 to 8 patties, about 3/4-inch thick, place on grill. For medium rare, cook about 4 minutes per side.

BBQ Clams and Fresh Tomato Sauce

(Serves 4)

- 18 ripe but firm plum tomatoes, peeled and seeded
- Extra virgin olive oil
- 5 medium garlic cloves
- 1/2 cup white wine
- Salt to taste
- 2 dozen clams (littleneck or cherrystone)

Place tomatoes in pot of boiling water for 20 seconds. Remove immediately and refresh with cold water. Open tomatoes with your fingers and remove seeds. Dice tomatoes. Cover bottom of saucepan with oil and place over medium heat. Sauté garlic until brown. Add diced tomatoes, white wine and salt to taste.

Wash clams, place on grill and cook 3 or 4 minutes. Clams are done when shells have opened. Remove from grill. Discard unopened clams.

Presto Pesto

- 2 cups basil leaves
- 1/2 cup Italian parsley
- 1 1/2 cups extra virgin olive oil
- 5 tablespoons pine nuts
- 4 cloves garlic
- Salt and pepper to taste
- 6 tablespoons fresh Parmesan

Put ingredients in food processor. When smooth, pour into bowl and fold in cheese.

Steakhouse Salad

- 2 heads iceberg lettuce

Remove outer leaves and cut into quarters. Rinse well, drain and set each quarter on a salad plate.

- 1 1/3 cups blue cheese, crumbled
- 4 tablespoons cider vinegar (or favorite wine vinegar)
- 1/2 cup salad oil
- Dash of garlic salt

Put cheese in small bowl. Add vinegar and gradually add oil, beating constantly with electric mixer or wire whisk.

Chipotle Cheese Dogs

For hot dogs, a real cheese fondue tastes weird. Fire up a can of Campbell's cheddar soup with a diced chipotle pepper. Serve in a fondue pot with a ladle.

Tang 'tinis

- 1/4 ounce Absolut Citron

- 1/4 ounce Triple Sec

- 1/4 cup Tang (dissolved)

Combine all ingredients in a cocktail shaker with ice, pour into chilled 'tini glass and garnish with an orange twist.

D'Andy Tomato Soup

- 2 cans Campbell's tomato soup

- 2 cans water

- 1/4 cup heavy cream

- 1/4 teaspoon vanilla

- 1 or 2 tablespoons sherry

Heat soup with water. Mix cream with vanilla and sherry. Refill the soup cans with doctored soup and garnish with a spoonful of sherried cream. Give the cream an op-art swiggle with the spoon handle.

Mo' Better Potato Chips

A memorable bar snack in minutes.

Preheat oven to 350 degrees F. Sprinkle plain potato chips on a baking sheet. Low-fat chips work, they're less greasy. Season with your favorite picks from the spice rack—black pepper, garlic powder, chili powder, paprika, a sprinkle of white vinegar, sea salt. Bake on cookie sheet for about 3 minutes until warmed and toss in bowl.

Better Than Bizness Class Nuts

Spicy-sweet, swift to make and, when served warm, really take off.

- 2 tablespoons butter
- 2 tablespoons sage, coarsely chopped, or fresh herb of choice
- 1/2 teaspoon cayenne pepper
- 2 teaspoons kosher salt
- 2 teaspoons dark brown sugar
- 3 pounds mixed unsalted nuts (cashews, peanuts, almonds, pistachios, whatever you like)

Preheat oven to 350 degrees F. Melt butter with spices and sugar. Toss mixed nuts and spread out on a cookie sheet and bake for about 10 minutes. Watch like a hawk. They go from golden to cinders in a flash. Alternatively, add nuts to spicy butter right in the pan and toast over medium-low heat until golden. Drain on paper towels.

Shrimp Cocktail

(Serves 6)

Precooked refrigerated shrimp from the supermarket is a bogus shortcut. The fish is usually bland, more expensive, and poaching shrimp at home is easy as boiling water. The only issue is peeling the shrimp, which is murder on your manicure—a nuisance before a party when your hands should look pretty shaking hands or drinks. Buy a pound of raw, peeled shrimp, then boil enough salted water to cover them. For extra credit, season the water with a splash of white wine, peppercorns, a thick slice of lemon. Simmer for 3 minutes or until shrimp turn pink. Serve with classic cocktail sauce or other dunkers.

Cocktail Sauce Classic

Jazzed-up ketchup.

- 1/2 cup ketchup
- 1/2 cup chili sauce
- 2 tablespoons fresh lemon juice
- 2 tablespoons horseradish
- Dash of Worcestershire sauce
- Salt
- Tabasco

Stir ingredients in a pretty glass bowl—a wine glass will do.

Green Sauce

Tons of herbs and homemade mayo.

- 2 cups mayonnaise
- 1 tablespoon chives, chopped
- 1 tablespoon tarragon, chopped
- 2 tablespoons parsley, chopped
- 1 teaspoon chervil, chopped
- 1 teaspoon dill, chopped

In a food processor, puree herbs. Fold into mayo, let stand two hours before serving.

Bango Mango

Puree 1/4 cup mango chutney with 1 cup mayonnaise.

Mayo-clinic

Now dissed as a plebian, cholesterol-loaded condiment, mayonnaise once had the culinary cachet of French sauce like béarnaise or hollandaise. But the homemade variety really has the same ingredients as a salad dressing and can be flavored and colored into many delish accompaniments to fish and raw veg.

- 2 egg yolks
- 1 teaspoon dry mustard
- 1 teaspoon salt
- Lemon or vinegar to taste
- 1 teaspoon sugar
- 2 cups olive oil
- 2 tablespoons vinegar or lemon

Mix egg yolks and seasoning in food processor, add oil a few drops at a time until mixture is thick and stiff. Thin with vinegar or lemon.

"Hot" Deviled Eggs

For a cocktail party we prefer this classic served hot, as in spicy and thirst-inducing. Edit out the Tabasco for any of the other variations.

- 6 eggs
- 1 teaspoon salt
- Dry mustard
- Worcestershire sauce
- 1/2 teaspoon ground pepper
- 1/4 teaspoon Tabasco
- 1 tablespoon mayonnaise

Boil eggs for 10 minutes, run under cold water. Peel and slice each egg in half. Remove yolks and force through a sieve. Add remaining ingredients.

Beat yolk mixture until pasty, add to pastry bag and fill egg white halves.

Anchovy Eggs

- 6 hard-boiled eggs
- 2 tablespoons anchovy paste (real ones are too hard to catch—and mash)
- 1/2 teaspoon ground pepper
- 1 teaspoon salt
- 1 tablespoon mayo

Remove yolks. Add anchovy paste, pepper, salt and mayo. Mix together and refill eggs.

Curried Eggs

- 6 hard-boiled eggs
- 1 teaspoon salt
- 2 teaspoons chutney, finely chopped
- 1 1/2 teaspoon curry powder
- 1 tablespoon mayo

Remove yolks of eggs. Add all ingredients, mix together and fill eggs. Top with shredded coconut.

Leftover alert: Add a wee bit of shredded cold chicken, shrimp or crab to the yolk mixture.

Less Crude Crudités

Make veggies seem more like a treat than a rabbit smorgasbord by serving fewer kinds and giving each more attention. Instead of a big bowl with a million vegetables and one dip, cut it down to two or three plates with just one vegetable on each and its own dip or spread or stuffing. And why do they always have to be raw?

Double-Stuffed Artichokes

(Makes 24)

- 12 baby artichokes
- 1/2 cup red wine vinegar
- 1 can artichoke hearts
- 1 cup mayonnaise
- 1 cup Parmesan
- Lemon juice (1 lemon, squeezed)
- Fresh pepper

Boil artichokes for 25 minutes in salted water with red wine vinegar. Drain and, when cool enough to handle, pull off the first few layers of leaves. With a super-sharp knife, cut the artichokes in half and remove the fuzzy choke with a melon baller.

Stuff the heart with more artichoke:

Preheat oven to 350 degrees F. Chop canned artichoke hearts, mix with mayo, Parmesan, lemon juice and pepper. In this retro classic dip, the mayo and cheese combine when cooked into a delicious dip with a pudding-like consistency you'd swear was breading. Fill chokes with the artichoke mixture. Bake for 15 minutes or until golden.

Party 'Shrooms

Anyone who's ever sautéed mushrooms knows they release a lot of water, which is why cooked mushroom caps are often mushy and slippery, the type of hors d'oeuvres you regret midway through. The raw cap, however, has a crunchy, fresher consistency and is just as good at holding stuffing like Roquefort spread.

- 1/2 pound Roquefort cheese
- 1/4 pound butter
- 1/4 pound cream cheese
- 1/2 teaspoon dry mustard
- 2 tablespoons cognac
- 2 tablespoons chopped mushroom stems
- Raisins and walnuts, finely chopped

Blend all ingredients together.

Canapés

Chicken Chutney

If you have leftover chicken, chop it in bits and add equal amounts of chutney and cream cheese, garnish with something nutty or fruity, like champagne grapes. Stir to make a smooth paste.

Tuna Bruschetta

A can of good Italian tuna packed in oil, a can of white beans (drained), a few pitted olives, black pepper. Mix with a fork or blend to a hummus-like paste. Spread on toast rounds and garnish with chopped tomato.

South of the Border Cocktail Time

Tropical Storm

- 2 ounces gold tequila
- 1/2 cup orange juice, freshly squeezed
- 1/2 cup Jamaica Flower Water, lime and orange slices

Fill a tall glass with ice, pour tequila, then OJ, then flower water. Float fruit on top.

Dale DeGroff's Blackberry Julep

- 1 1/2 ounces Marie Brizard blackberry liqueur
- 3/4 ounce fresh lemon juice
- 3/4 ounce simple syrup

Shake all the ingredients with 1 ounce water and ice. Strain into a highball glass three-quarters filled with crushed ice. Garnish with heaping tablespoon Mixed Marinated Berries and serve with a straw.

Corn on the Cob with Cayenne and Lime

- 6 ears corn
- 6 tablespoons unsalted butter
- 1 1/2 teaspoons cayenne pepper
- 2 tablespoons lime juice
- 1 teaspoon salt

Cut corn into 3-inch party lengths. Bring a large pot of salted water to boil, add corn and turn off heat. Melt butter with cayenne pepper; add lime and salt. Brush corn with spicy butter and serve.

Garnish: Mixed Marinated Berries

- 1 pint blueberries, strawberries, and black and red raspberries
- 2 teaspoons brandy
- 4 teaspoons Cointreau
- 2 tablespoons sugar

Steep berries, brandy, Cointreau and sugar for 3 hours.

One Dish Wonders

Bouillabaisse

- 3 tablespoons olive oil
- 1 tablespoon unsalted butter
- 1 medium leek
- 1 small fennel bulb
- 1 medium celery stalk
- 1 bay leaf
- Peel of 1/2 orange
- 1/4 teaspoon saffron threads
- 1/2 teaspoon sea salt
- 3 cloves minced garlic
- 1 tablespoon tomato paste
- 1/2 cup dry white wine
- 1 1/2 cups canned whole tomatoes with juice, broken into pieces
- 2 cups of fish stock (or fish bouillon)
- 1/2 teaspoon ground red pepper
- 3/4 teaspoon salt
- 12 littleneck clams

- 3/4 pound sea bass, or halibut fillets (cut into 1 1/2 pieces)
- 12 sea scallops

Heat 1 tablespoon olive oil and butter in a large saucepan over medium heat. Add chopped vegetables, bay leaf, orange peel, saffron and salt. Cook until tender but not browned. Add garlic and cook for two minutes before stirring in tomato paste. Give it a minute then pour in the wine and allow to boil for a few minutes. Now in go the tomatoes, fish broth and red pepper. This is the bouillabaisse broth. Let simmer for twenty minutes. Meanwhile, in a separate soup pot heat 2 tablespoons olive oil and add clams. Cook, stirring for a few minutes, then add broth. Bring it to a boil, then lower heat to a simmer and add the fish, followed by the scallops. Cook for about three minutes more. Chuck any clams that didn't open. Serve with toasted bread. Voilà.

Choucroute Garni

This sweet, savory Alsatian dish is sort of like hot dogs for grown-ups. The main thing is to go to a butcher and get a good variety of smoked meats and sausages. Bavarian beer-garden party.

- 2 pounds sauerkraut
- 1/2 pound bacon, coarsely diced
- 1 yellow onion, chopped
- 1 carrot, chopped
- Brandy
- 1 cooking apple, grated
- 1 tablespoon caraway seeds
- 1 cup Alsatian wine
- 4 cups chicken stock

- 6 peppercorns

- 2 bay leaves

- 6 smoked pork chops, or smoked duck

- 1 1/2 pounds sausage (bratwurst, knockwurst, polish sausage, whatever looks good)

- 4 parsley sprigs, chopped

- 6 small boiled potatoes, cut in half

Soak kraut in a bowl of cold water for 30 minutes. Meanwhile, preheat oven to 325 degrees F. Slice bacon crossways and fry the bits. Drain, but don't clean the pan. Lightly brown onion and carrots, add drained kraut and sauté in remaining drippings. In go the brandy, apple and caraway seeds, and cook a few minutes longer. Pour in the wine and enough chicken stock to cover the kraut. Tie all the spices up in a cheesecloth bag and toss in the casserole. Add the smoky chops and sausages and cook in the oven for 3 hours. Sprinkle parsley over the potatoes.

"Big Night" Lasagna

Tiny meatballs baked into the noodle casserole give this lasagna more dinner party elegance, or at least make it less sloppy.

(Serves 10)

- 1 pound lean chopped meat

- 3 tablespoons salt

- 1/4 teaspoon pepper

- 5 tablespoons grated pecorino Romano

- 1 large egg

- Fresh parsley, chopped

- Stale loaf of Italian bread, about 12 inches

- 2 tablespoons olive oil

- vegetable oil

- 1 pound fresh ricotta

- 1 pound lasagna, cooked and drained

- 3 cups tomato sauce

- 1 pound fresh salted mozzarella, sliced

- 1 1/2 cups fresh grated Parmesan cheese

Start with meatballs: Season beef with salt, pepper, cheese, egg, a few shakes of parsley. Soak bread in warm water, and when soft, scoop out the white, discard the crust, add to meat and mix well. Roll into marble-size balls and brown in hot olive oil for about 6 minutes. A meatball that sticks to the pan is not ready to be turned.

Fill a large pasta pot or soup kettle with water, bring to a rapid boil, add 3 tablespoons salt and vegetable oil. Preheat oven to 350 degrees F. Put ricotta cheese into a bowl, add approximately 4 tablespoons sauce and mix, giving the ricotta color and flavor. Set aside. Place lasagna into boiling water one noodle at a time. Mix with a wooden spoon, allow to boil, mixing from time to time.

While pasta is cooking, cover a large flat surface with paper towels. When pasta is ready, bring pot to sink, pour off some water and continue to add cold water until you are able to take out lasagna with your hands, removing excess water with fingers. Place on paper towels and dab dry.

Cover bottom of baking pan with tomato sauce. Add a layer of lasagna, allowing each noodle to slightly overlap the next. Add a layer of sauce, a few spoonfuls of ricotta cheese, some meatballs, mozzarella pieces and Parmesan. Add next layer of lasagna; cover with sauce, ricotta and so forth until there is no more pasta. On the top layer of lasagna put sauce and Parmesan cheese.

Bake for 1 hour. Cut portions in squares and serve.

Boeuf Bourguignon

- 1/2 pound small mushrooms
- 2 tablespoons butter
- 2 cups Burgundy wine
- 2 tablespoons lard
- 4 ounces salt pork, diced
- 3 pounds shoulder beef, cut into 2-inch squares
- 3 tablespoons flour
- 2 cloves garlic
- 1 tablespoon parsley, chopped
- Orange peel, 2-inch piece
- 1 bay leaf
- 1/4 tablespoon thyme
- 1/4 tablespoon nutmeg
- 1 teaspoon salt
- 12 shallots

Trim ugly part of stem off mushrooms and sauté in butter whole—they're for garnishing. Heat wine in a separate saucepan. In a big casserole or pot heat the lard. When it begins to smoke, turn on the fan, open the windows and add the salt pork. Brown and remove. Dredge the beef cubes in flower and brown in pan. Add back the salt pork and wine, garlic, parsley, orange peel and spices.

That's it. Now cover tightly and cook over low heat for 3 1/2 hours. Remove cover, add shallots and cook another 15 minutes. Remove orange and garlic. Garnish with the mushrooms.

Candied Carrots

- 18 small peeled carrots
- Salt
- Water
- 6 tablespoons butter, melted
- 1/2 cup brown sugar

Place carrots in pan, cover with salt water, bring to a boil and cook until tender with a fork. Preheat oven to 350 degrees F. Drain carrots and transfer to a shallow casserole. Coat with melted butter and sprinkle with brown sugar. Bake 15 minutes or until glazed.

Chic Peas

- 1 small head Boston lettuce, shredded
- 2 packages frozen small peas, or 4 cups fresh
- 4 sprigs parsley
- 1/2 teaspoon salt
- 1/4 teaspoon sugar
- 1 teaspoon thyme
- 1/4 cup butter
- 2 tablespoons water
- 1 tablespoon green onion, finely chopped

Place lettuce in a saucepan first. Then add the rest of the ingredients, bring to a boil, stir, lower heat and simmer, covered, for 10 minutes.

French Salad

(Serves 6)

- 2 tablespoons red wine vinegar

- 6 tablespoons olive oil

- 1/4 teaspoon salt

- 1/4 teaspoon pepper, freshly ground

- 1/2 teaspoon Dijon or a dash of dry mustard

- Fresh tarragon, chervil or basil

- 1 head Boston or bibb lettuce

Traditional French salads turn up their nose at balsamic vinegar. Red wine vinegar makes for a lighter yet more savory dressing. Mix the dressing in the bottom of your salad bowl and add lettuce. Secret: for the best salad, dry the greens and chill them in the fridge before tossing. Serve dressing at room temperature.

Boozy Starters

Gazpacholé

Aunt Paca's recipe from La Mancha is as simple and authentic as it gets.

- 6 ripe tomatoes

- 1 cucumber

- 1 green pepper, seeded and diced

- 1 sweet onion, or 1 Spanish onion

- 1 garlic clove, crushed

- 1 teaspoon salt

- Black pepper

- 1/2 teaspoon paprika

- 1/2 cup water, or stock

- 1/4 cup olive oil

- 1/4 cup red wine vinegar

(For more liquid add tomato juice)

- Bread crumbs (who knows how much)

Blend all ingredients in blender and chill 2 to 3 hours. Serve in bowls and pass around a chilled bottle of *pepper-flavored vodka.*

Home-Flavored Vodka

Open a favorite brand and pour off a shot for yourself. Now you have enough room to plop in the rind from a lemon peel or a handful of peppercorns, raspberries or vanilla beans. Let the bottle marinate for a few days to a week. Turn the bottle every now and then.

Hiccup Fruit Cocktail

You need a melon baller, a crisper full of seasonal fruits and a couple of bottles for marinating. Rum-soaked pineapple balls with strawberries. Cherry halves and peach slices in cognac. Fresh plums and apricots in brandy. Then mix together, happy-hour style, and serve in ample martini glasses.

I Scream Ice Cream Cake

Make your own to rival Fudgie the Whale. Just get a 9-inch springform pan, about 6 pints of your favorite ice cream and 2 cups of crushed cookie or candy.

Spread 2 pints of softened ice cream per layer, sprinkle with chopped candy, repeat until the pan is filled, ending with an ice cream layer. Place in freezer.

Blue-Ribbon Mac 'n' Cheese

(Serves 8)

- Salt
- 1/2 cup macaroni
- 1/2 pound chopped meat
- 1 small onion, diced
- 2 cans tomatoes
- 1 tablespoon ketchup, or tomato juice
- Pepper
- 3 cups Cheese Sauce
- 3 or 4 slices bread, brown or white
- 3 tablespoons butter

Boil salted water and add macaroni. While cooking, brown chopped meat in skillet with onion on medium heat. Add something tomato-y—tomatoes and ketchup or tomato juice—then mix with meat. Add salt and pepper. Put in bottom of casserole. Add strained noodles to casserole, then pour Cheese Sauce. Put aside and make bread crumbs.

Grind bread in food processor. Melt 3 tablespoons butter and toss around bread bits until coated in butter. (They'll crisp in the oven.) Sprinkle on top of casserole, and heat at 375 degrees F. for about 1/2 hour or until golden brown and bubbling.

Cheese Sauce:

- 3 tablespoons butter
- 6 tablespoons flour
- 3 cups milk
- Cracker Barrel cheese, extra sharp, grated

Over medium heat, melt butter, stir in flour, add milk. Stir until the sauce begins to thicken and add grated cheese bit by bit until melted.

Super Sundae

To make one giant group sundae, fill a punch bowl with pints of your favorite ice creams. Top with nuts and sprinkles and cherries and bananas and pink whipped cream. People scoop their own and top their sundae with their choice of sundae sauces (see below), warming in fondue pots.

Pink Whipped Cream

Whip 3 pints heavy cream with 3 tablespoons Grenadine.

Sundae Sauces

Rummy Chocolate Sauce

- 4 ounces unsweetened chocolate
- 3 tablespoons sweet butter
- 2/3 cup water
- 1 2/3 cups sugar
- 6 tablespoons corn syrup
- 1 tablespoon rum

Melt chocolate and butter on low heat, then add boiling water and stir. Add sugar and corn syrup and mix until smooth. Turn heat up and stir until boils; allow sauce to boil for just under 10 minutes. Remove sauce from heat and cool 15 minutes. Stir in rum.

Raspberry Sauce

- 1 package (12 ounces) frozen raspberries
- 3 tablespoons sugar

Thaw raspberries. Press through fine sieve or whirl in blender; strain. Add sugar. Dissolve in saucepan over medium heat; cook rapidly for 3 minutes.

Butterscotch Sauce Fondue

- 1/2 cup butter or margarine
- 2 cups brown sugar
- 1 cup light corn syrup
- 2 tablespoons water
- 1 1/3 cups sweetened condensed milk
- 1 teaspoon vanilla

Melt butter. Stir in sugar, corn syrup and water. Bring to boil. Add milk, lower heat and simmer, stirring constantly until reaches 230 degrees F. Add vanilla, and pour into fondue pot.

Nutsy Fondue

- One 6-ounce package semisweet chocolate pieces
- 1/2 cup sugar
- 1/2 cup milk
- 1/2 cup chunky peanut butter

Combine chocolate pieces, sugar and milk in saucepan over medium heat. Stir constantly until melted. Add peanut butter. Mix well. Transfer to fondue pot.

Easy as Pie Night

Clem Rowley's no-fail recipe. She doubles it to top the pie.

- 1 1/2 cups flour
- 1/2 teaspoon salt
- 3 tablespoons ice water
- 1/2 cup Crisco

Sift flour and salt.

Take 1/4 cup flour out and stir with ice water until it makes a paste in a little tea cup or something you can set aside. Blend remaining flour and Crisco until crumbly. Add just enough flour/water mixture so you can bunch the dough into a ball, wrap it in wax paper and stick it in the fridge. (Overhandling the dough at this point will make it less flaky.)

While dough is chilling, make fruit filling.

Fruit Filling:
- 5 to 7 apples (Rome or Granny Smith), peeled, cored and sliced
- 3/4 cup sugar
- 2 tablespoons flour
- dash salt
- 1 teaspoon cinnamon
- 1/4 teaspoon nutmeg

Mix everything. Preheat oven to 400 degrees F. Roll out pie dough between two pieces of wax paper. Flip the crust into a pie plate; fill with fruit. Roll out another crust, and cover. Crimp the edges together. Make a couple slits on top for steam to escape. Sprinkle with sugar. One tip from Clem: Take a few strips of aluminum foil and cover edge of crust so it doesn't blacken. Bake for 50 minutes.

Even Easier Pie:

If you lost your rolling pin chasing that man out of your house, you can still make a crust with vanilla or chocolate wafers or ginger snaps.

- 1 1/2 cups fine wafer crumbs
- 6 tablespoons melted butter

Mix wafer crumbs and melted butter. Press into a 9-inch pie plate. Chill while making filling.

Pretty Cake, Pretty Cake

Frosted Lemon Pound Cake:

- 4 eggs
- 1 package yellow cake mix
- 1 package lemon pudding mix
- 3/4 cup water
- 1/3 cup salad oil
- Lemon Glaze

Preheat oven to 350 degrees F. Beat eggs until thick. Add cake mix and pudding mix, water and oil. Beat 10 minutes at medium speed and pour into an ungreased 10-inch tube pan. Bake for 50 minutes. Drizzle Lemon Glaze over top and spread on sides of cake. Cool completely.

Lemon Glaze:

- 2 cups sifted confectioners' sugar
- 1/3 cup lemon juice

Heat confectioners' sugar and lemon juice to boiling.

Not Cheese Bored

Sandwich Cookies:

Remove rind from a wedge of Brie, and whip cheese with electric mixer for about 10 minutes until light and creamy. Pastry bag or spoon cheese onto crackers or ginger snaps and cover with a second cookie to complete the sandwich.

Freak-out Frico:

Amazingly simple delicate cheese crisps that accompany cocktails in Friuli—northern Italy. There they are made with Mantasio, which is like a fine cheddar, but you can do it with a good Parmesan or any great grate-able cheese. (Serves 6)

- 1 1/2 teaspoons polenta flour
- 1 cup grated cheese

Heat a good nonstick 9-inch frying pan on medium, then sprinkle with 1/2 teaspoon flour followed quickly by 1/3 cup grated cheese, as evenly as you can. Cook for about 1 1/2 minutes. Loosen the wafer with a spatula. Remove pan from heat and let rest a minute before turning the frico, cooking the other side for another minute. Put the frico on a serving platter. Wipe pan clean with a paper towel and keep going. They're good for a few hours.

Apple Tartlets (with cheddar topping):

- 2 green apples, peeled, cored and sliced
- 2 tablespoons light brown sugar
- 1 tablespoon honey
- 1/4 teaspoon cinnamon
- 1/2 teaspoon lemon rind
- 1 tablespoon butter
- Frozen pastry cups
- 1/4 cup grated sharp cheddar cheese

Preheat oven to 325 degrees F. Melt apples and seasoning over low heat in a saucepan until apples are soft but still hold their shape. Fill pastry cups and sprinkle with cheddar cheese. Bake for 5 minutes or until cheese is melted.

How to Give Toasts

Another way to liven up the cheese bored is to lose the crackers and make your own toasts by slicing up a baguette or brioche into rounds or triangles, about 1/4 inch thick.

Preheat oven to 300 degrees F. Place bread slices on baking sheet and drizzle or brush with olive oil. Sprinkle lightly with salt. Bake for 10 to 15 minutes or until golden.

Caviar Dream Puffs

They're made from pâté à choux, a very basic dough that can be filled with savory or sweet fillings, from caviar to ice cream. Puffs are a simple cooking project, and well worth the effort. Particularly if you make it the only cooking you do—just puffs from appetizers to dessert. And you can make the cream puff shells a week before your party, freeze them and just fill them the day of.

(Makes a dozen)

- 1 cup water
- 6 tablespoons butter
- 1/8 teaspoon pepper
- 1 teaspoon salt
- 3/4 cup flour
- 5 eggs

Bring water to a boil with butter and pepper and salt. Boil slowly until butter has melted.

Remove from heat and pour in flour. Beat with wooden spoon to blend, then beat over medium heat for 2 minutes, until mixture congeals and separates from pan. Remove from heat and make a well in the center of the paste with wooden spoon. Break an egg into the well. Beat egg into paste, and add three more eggs one by one until paste is smooth.

Preheat oven to 425 degrees F. Drop spoonfuls of dough onto 2 nonstick baking sheets, about 1 inch wide and 1/2 inch tall. They will double in size as you bake them, so give them plenty of spreading-out room.

Flatten each mound with the pastry brush dipped in a beaten egg.

Now the baking, the complicated part. Place baking sheets in oven for 20 minutes until puffs are lightly browned. Lower heat to 375 and bake 15 minutes more, or until the puffs are crusty to the touch. Hot puffs may look perfect when pulled from the oven, but the insides are often still moist and if left to cool will get soggy. To keep them dry, when pulled from the oven, puncture the puffs and return them to a turned-off oven that's still warm where they can dry for 10 minutes. Use a pastry bag to fill puffs.

Marshmallow in Chocolate Fondue

Why bother making your own marshmallows when a bag can last 40 years in your cupboard? Because it's easy and you can cut them into your own shapes or flavor and color and decorate with candy.

- 1 envelope unflavored gelatin
- 1/3 cup cold water
- 1/2 cup sugar
- 2/3 cup light corn syrup
- 1/2 teaspoon vanilla extract
- Cornstarch

Soften gelatin in cold water and dissolve over low heat. Add sugar and stir until dissolved. In a large mixing bowl, add gelatin, corn syrup and vanilla, beat at high speed for 15 minutes, or until mixture is marshmallow consistency. Pour into a 9 x 9-inch pan dusted with equal parts sugar and cornstarch. Pour in marshmallow mixture. Let stand in a cool place for 1 hour. Loosen from pan and turn onto a board or wax paper sprinkled with cornstarch and sugar. Cut into shapes you dig and roll in sugar-cornstarch again.

Enjoy!